THE BEST COURTS MONEY COULD BUY

THE BEST COURTS MONEY COULD BUY

REFORM OF THE OKLAHOMA JUDICIARY 1956–1967

LEE CARD

UNIVERSITY OF OKLAHOMA PRESS : NORMAN

This book is published with the generous assistance of the Wallace C. Thompson Endowment Fund, University of Oklahoma Foundation.

Library of Congress Cataloging-in-Publication Data

Names: Card, Lee Arthur, 1950– author.
Title: The best courts money could buy : reform of the Oklahoma judiciary, 1956–1967 / Lee Card.
Description: First. | Norman : University of Oklahoma Press, 2020. | Based on author's thesis (doctoral—University of Oklahoma, 2016) issued under title: Scandal and reform: a historical study of corruption and reform in Oklahoma's court system, 1956–1967. | Includes bibliographical references and index.
Identifiers: LCCN 2020006485 | ISBN 978-0-8061-6631-5 (paperback)
Subjects: LCSH: Judicial corruption—Oklahoma—History—20th century. | Justice, Administration of—Oklahoma—History—20th century. | Oklahoma—Politics and government—20th century.
Classification: LCC KFO1725.5.D5 C37 2020 | DDC 347.766/01—dc23
LC record available at https://lccn.loc.gov/2020006485

The paper in this book meets the guidelines for permanence and durability of the Committee on Production Guidelines for Book Longevity of the Council on Library Resources, Inc. ∞

Copyright © 2020 by the University of Oklahoma Press, Norman, Publishing Division of the University. Manufactured in the U.S.A.

All rights reserved. No part of this publication may be reproduced, stored in a retrieval system, or transmitted, in any form or by any means, electronic, mechanical, photocopying, recording, or otherwise—except as permitted under Section 107 or 108 of the United States Copyright Act—without the prior written permission of the University of Oklahoma Press. To request permission to reproduce selections from this book, write to Permissions, University of Oklahoma Press, 2800 Venture Drive, Norman OK 73069, or email rights. oupress@ou.edu.

This book is dedicated to my wife, Debbie. She has encouraged me in this endeavor, has proofread my writing, and has put up with messy papers and scattered documents all over our house. She has been an inspiration to me, and I can never thank her enough.

This book is also dedicated to the Oklahoma lawyers of the 1960s who skillfully guided the process of exposing a terrible scandal and reforming a broken judicial system. They overcame the humiliation suffered by the legal profession and created a judiciary of which Oklahoma can be proud.

Finally, this book is dedicated to my dad, William L. Card, and my uncle G. M. Fuller. Both were Oklahoma lawyer-legislators who served their state honestly, honorably, and capably. I am proud and honored to be part of their family.

Contents

		Introduction	1
❖	1	A System in Need of Reform	5
❖	2	The State of the Court	25
❖	3	Prosecution and the Seeds of Reform	39
❖	4	The 1965 Legislature and the Impeachment of N. B. Johnson	62
❖	5	The Fall of McCarty, the Sneed Plan, and the Election of 1966	81
❖	6	The Enactment of Legislative Reform and Defeat of the Sneed Plan	99
❖	7	Oklahoma after Court Reform	115
		Notes	131
		Bibliography	149
		Index	155

Introduction

Between 1956 and 1967 Oklahoma experienced a catastrophic bribery scandal at the highest level of the state's judiciary. Oklahomans learned to their horror that, in exchange for cash, justices of the Oklahoma Supreme Court decided cases in favor of the highest bidder, and that this practice had existed for many years. Exposure of the scandal led to the successful prosecutions of those responsible and, after skillful political maneuvering by the state's political leadership, to significant reform in Oklahoma's judicial system. This book is a history of these events written to educate younger generations about what happened.

As time has passed, the judicial scandal and reform have faded from the state's collective political memory. To the extent they are remembered at all, the events offer a picture of the brazen nature of the crimes and the shameless, long-standing criminality of men in positions of power in the worlds of law, politics, and business. If we look past the surface drama of the scandal, the bribery conforms to a narrative of corrupt politics that is a part of mid-twentieth-century southern U.S. history. Large personalities and extravagant courtroom theatrics are integral to one-party systems in which issue debate is rare and many important policy decisions are made behind closed doors by the economic and political elite.

Oklahoma had been a state for only a half century when the most flagrant of these crimes were committed. Anglo-American immigration to Indian Territory in sizable numbers had commenced only after the Civil War, while Oklahoma Territory had been open for white settlement for less than twenty years when statehood was granted in 1907. Like all frontiers, Oklahoma reflected the backgrounds and cultures of its new inhabitants. Its political leadership in particular reflected influences of the West, the South, and its large Native American population.

In nostalgically thinking of early Oklahoma as a western frontier, we often overlook its position as a geographic, political, and cultural borderland of the South. Despite the distinctive presence of a Native American population involuntarily assigned to federally designated "Indian Country," many of the new white settlers, most of them native southerners, envisioned the new state in which "white over black" was the strongest social and political assumption. Early Oklahoma was a place where people of energy and intelligence could improve their lot in life. However, the absence of established governmental and cultural rules also offered opportunities for devious, outsized personalities to exploit others for their own benefit. Hundreds or thousands of Native Americans lost their allotments to hucksters and embezzlers. A generation later, O. A. Cargill, N. S. Corn, Hugh Carroll, and others would continue this practice of exploiting governmental weakness for personal financial gain.

For the most part, Oklahoma's constitution was written by white men with southern backgrounds. In crafting that document, the drafters relied enormously on the advice of populist Democrat William Jennings Bryan. Populism, a political movement that was fading in other sections of the country, still thrived in Oklahoma in 1907, and the constitution, including its judicial framework, reflected that school of political thought, as well as progressivism. One of populism's features, a long ballot with most state officials chosen by the electorate, played a significant role in the scandal that came a half-century later. In addition, Oklahoma adopted the southern propensity for penury when it came to paying public employees, thus being penny-wise and pound-foolish. Oklahoma's government paid judges poorly and relied on the cheap, but obsolete and discredited, justice of the peace system for routine cases.

The judicial scandal and subsequent reform deserve serious historical attention, for they had a permanent effect on Oklahoma's political and legal landscape. I first explore the weaknesses of the political and legal system that allowed the scandal to occur. Next, I outline the efforts to expose graft at the highest level of Oklahoma's court system, the resistance to the enactment of judicial reform, and the demonstration of extraordinary political skill and leadership in the 1967 passage of the constitutional amendments that achieved that reform.

At this period in the state's history, lawyers dominated the state's political structure. Many of the legislators who championed and ultimately enacted judicial reform were attorneys, who made up the largest single occupation represented in the legislature. Lawyers encouraged the movement for reform, with hundreds of them acting bravely and capably in fixing a corrupt and broken system. In addition, I also discuss the inherent potential conflict between being a part-time legislator and a full-time lawyer. Most lawyer-legislators served their constituents honorably and ethically, using their legal training and experience to draft and pass legislation that benefited the state and their districts. Some lawyer-legislators, certainly not most, abused their state office for the gain of their clients and themselves, blurring or ignoring the line between representing their clients and representing their districts.

The magnitude of the bribery scandal gradually became clear during the years between 1963 and 1965. By the time the scope of the crimes was known, the men who had committed them had become elderly and infirm. The bribery scandal centered around five men: Justices Nelson S. Corn, Earl Welch, and N. B. Johnson; attorney O. A. Cargill; and businessman Hugh Carroll. All five had come to maturity in the challenging frontier world of statehood-era Oklahoma. All were self-educated, had overcome poverty, and had, through intelligence and ambition, achieved positions of power, public respect, and responsibility. All five, however, descended into the ugly and corrupt business of influence peddling and bribery, betraying those who had trusted them. Defects in Oklahoma's political and judicial systems helped provide the opportunity for these men to perpetrate these crimes.

Although corruption certainly occurred in many other Supreme Court cases of the time, officials conclusively proved bribery in only three cases: *Oklahoma Tax Commission v. Selected Investments*, *Marshall v. Amos*, and *Oklahoma Company v. O'Neil*. *Marshall v. Amos* and *Oklahoma Company v. O'Neil* both involved oil and gas production; in the latter case, O. A. Cargill's daughter and son-in-law were litigants with an enormous stake in the outcome. A fourth case, *Meadors*, involved misconduct as well, though one of the leading actors in that case, Justice Ben Arnold, died before the scandal was exposed. By far the most spectacular and egregious of the cases was *Selected Investments*, which involved financial and legal misconduct on a monumental and unprecedented scale.

The changes brought by reform were far-reaching and completely changed Oklahoma's court system. Voters narrowly approved the establishment of the Judicial Nominating Commission and the creation of the Court on the Judiciary to deal with judicial misconduct. They also voted to centralize the state's court system, placing district courts under the control of the Supreme Court and a statewide court administrator.

The reforms also greatly improved judicial selection. For its first fifty years, like many states, Oklahoma elected its judges on a partisan ballot, in which the candidate identified himself by political party. In a one-party state like Oklahoma, this meant the winner of the Democratic Party's nomination nearly always won the election, particularly in judicial elections, which had few issues and generally little voter interest. The 1967 constitutional amendments changed the electoral process, initiating a referendum for appellate judges in which the electorate decides whether an appellate judge should be retained in office. After the enactment of reform, trial judges ran in contested elections, but without the party affiliation of the candidates being disclosed.

Structurally, the reform also abolished the obsolete and ineffective office of justice of the peace (JP) and replaced the antiquated county attorney system with the district attorney system. Oklahomans replaced justices of the peace with the position of special district judge, a nonelected professional jurist with considerably more power, prestige, and professionalism than the JPs. With a few modifications, these changes remain in place today. As of this writing, however, some of these reforms—especially Oklahoma's retention system for appellate judges and the Judicial Nominating Commission—are under fire from critics. Change may come yet again.

❖ 1
A System in Need of Reform

On January 21, 1965, thirty-six-year-old Republican representative G. T. Blankenship rose to address the Oklahoma House of Representatives on a matter of personal privilege. In the next few minutes Blankenship stunned Oklahoma's political landscape by exposing the largest judicial scandal in the state's history. Blankenship began his remarks by stating his concern as a legislator and lawyer for what he was going to say. Next to a house of worship, Blankenship said, courtrooms were the epitome of sacred institutions. He declared that honest judges deserved to have the tarnish of their reputations removed and outlined the importance of public confidence in the judicial process.

Blankenship then told the House that he had seen a copy of an exhaustive, eighty-two-page confession that former Oklahoma Supreme Court justice Nelson S. Corn had given to federal and state authorities on December 2, 1964, approximately six weeks previously. The eighty-year-old Corn had provided this information from a federal prison in Springfield, Missouri, for infirm inmates, where he was confined for income tax evasion. Corn confessed that he had accepted bribes in at least two cases in his time on the court, and that Justices Earl Welch and Napoleon Bonaparte (N. B.) Johnson, as well as an Oklahoma lawyer whom Blankenship identified only as "Mister X," had also been involved. One of those cases involved a favorable decision for Selected Investments, a corrupt investments company whose notorious and spectacular failure had startled and terrified investors, many of them Oklahomans, seven years before Blankenship's speech. Although Blankenship did not vouch for the truth of Corn's statement, he pointed out that there was no question that Corn had made the claims. It was, therefore, according to Representative Blankenship, the duty of the legislature to investigate, clear the innocent, and renew the public's faith in the court system.[1]

G. T. Blankenship had made a great speech at enormous personal risk. Legislative immunity notwithstanding, a practicing attorney had just accused three Oklahoma Supreme Court justices, two of whom were still in office, and a lawyer of bribery. In addition to their other duties, the Oklahoma Supreme

Court handled lawyer licensing matters. Although the situations were admittedly different, Blankenship would have been aware of the fate of Harlan Grimes, a lawyer who had questioned the integrity of the Supreme Court in *Marshall v. Amos*, another case in which Corn admitted bribery, and had been disbarred. Governor Henry Bellmon, worried about Blankenship, summoned his fellow Republican to his office and warned him of stormy seas ahead.[2]

As a Republican, Blankenship could expect little support from the legislative leadership. Despite significant court-ordered reapportionment, only twenty-two of the ninety-nine members of the House of Representatives were Republicans; the state Senate was even more disproportionate, with forty-one of the forty-eight seats occupied by Democrats. Corn, Welch, and Johnson, the three justices Blankenship identified as corrupt, all had been elected to the Supreme Court as Democrats. The powerful Speaker of the House, J. D. McCarty, was a Democrat, as was the legislative leadership.

The investigation of the court scandal confirmed what had been suspected for years: the votes of some members of the Oklahoma Supreme Court could be purchased with bribes. As events unfolded, Oklahoma's citizens learned that their government was alarmingly susceptible to favoritism and backroom deals. Two years later, with the assistance of able and astute political leadership, Oklahomans reformed their court system. In this book, my aim is to describe the environment that led to the scandal, the scandal itself, the public reaction, and the institution of judicial reform.

Oklahoma's Political Establishment Fifty Years after Statehood

In 1907 Oklahoma became a state, having combined the "twins," Oklahoma Territory and Indian Territory. For the next fifty years certain common themes appear in Oklahoma's political history. First, Oklahoma was a one-party state, with the Democratic Party dominating the political landscape. Until Republican Henry Bellmon's 1962 election, every Oklahoma governor had been a Democrat. Oklahomans elected three Republicans to the U.S. Senate, each of whom served only one term. With the exceptions of setbacks in 1920 and 1928, when the Democratic ticket was led by unpopular presidential candidates, Democrats dominated the down-ballot offices as well. While Republicans were very competitive in northwestern Oklahoma and, in later years, Tulsa, statewide Democrats outnumbered Republicans overwhelmingly.

Writing at approximately the same time as the Oklahoma court scandal occurred, political scientist V. O. Key Jr. discussed the effect that a one-party system has on the party in power. Key argued, "Lacking opposition, no external pressure drives the party toward internal unity and discipline. . . . The party organization, therefore, becomes merely a framework for intraparty factional and personal competition. It has the usual complement of conventions, committees, and officials, but the resemblance to genuine party organization is purely formal."[3] This occurred in Oklahoma in its first half-century. Democrats, the dominant party, fought bitterly with each other. Being a Democrat meant little in terms of sharing a political philosophy or a common platform.

Some of the tension came from conflict between the legislature and the governor. Governors invariably entered office with widespread voter popularity and ambitious agendas. However, since they were legally limited to only one term in office, they were lame ducks from the day of their inaugurations. With very few exceptions, the governors met vociferous resistance from the legislature, and most governors left office disappointed.[4] Legislators impeached and removed from office two governors, Jack Walton and Henry S. Johnston. Walton, who fell victim to a combination of his own abusive and bizarre behavior and a legislature dominated by the Ku Klux Klan, was removed in 1923 after less than a year in office. Johnston, who had unnecessarily created enemies in the capitol by ignoring legislators, was removed in 1929 by a combination of Democratic enemies in the legislature and an unusually high and effective number of Republican legislators, elected as a reaction to Al Smith's wildly unpopular 1928 Democratic presidential nomination. Although Johnston was indeed a poor governor with little executive ability, his removal from office was unnecessary and stands as an example of the excessive power of Oklahoma's legislature.[5]

The legislature itself was disproportionately rural. Although the state constitution required that the legislature be reapportioned every ten years, that mandate went ignored. The House of Representatives had not reapportioned itself since 1921, and the Senate had never done so. Each county, regardless of population, was guaranteed one member in the House of Representatives. Although the state became considerably more urban in the post–World War II years, rural legislators retained a power far disproportionate to the population of their districts. By 1962, when the U.S. Supreme Court addressed the issue in *Baker v. Carr* and subsequent cases, only three state legislatures were apportioned more disproportionately than Oklahoma's.[6] In the state's voting patterns, the differences between rural and urban manifested themselves again and again.

A high percentage of legislators were lawyers. Most of these lawyer-legislators were young attorneys seeking to serve the public, gain experience, and increase name recognition in their communities. For some, however, a seat in the legislature provided an opportunity to craft and enact legislation favoring their private legal clients, thus creating an incentive for private companies desiring some assistance from the legislature to hire lawyer-legislators as their attorney. For those lawyer-legislators, the ethical line between representing the interests of their legislative districts and those of their legal clients could become fuzzy.

Oklahoma's demographics were indeed changing drastically, as its citizens abandoned agriculture for the cities. Grant County, located on the Kansas border, had a population of more than 18,000 people in 1910. By 1950 the number had dropped to 10,461, and by 1970 only 7,117 people lived in Grant County.[7] Statewide, the percentage of people employed in agriculture plummeted from 33 percent in 1940 to 5 percent in 1970. During the 1950s alone, the number of farms plunged from 142,000 to 95,000.[8] By contrast, Oklahoma's cities were growing exponentially. Between 1910 and 1950 the population of Oklahoma County grew from 116,307 to 325,352; over the next twenty years, the county's numbers increased to 526,805. Tulsa County, Comanche County, and Cleveland County all experienced similar increases.[9]

Hundreds of scholars have described the brutality, inequities, and humiliations of segregation, a practice that Oklahoma adopted and maintained. The state's constitution mandated segregated schools, and the first legislature ordered separate public facilities and transportation, "which shall be equal in all points of comfort and convenience."[10] Courthouses were segregated, making the symbol of the blindfolded Lady Justice more ironic than iconic. In the 1920s the Ku Klux Klan became a leading force in Oklahoma politics, dominating the state's legislature and leading to the impeachment of a governor. In 1921 an attempt to lynch a black rape suspect in Tulsa led to the bloodiest riot in state history, in which the prosperous black Greenwood neighborhood was destroyed. During the 1950s, when most of the judicial scandal occurred, segregation still gripped Oklahoma. By the mid-1960s, when the corruption in the courts was exposed and reform enacted, the federal government had abolished segregation throughout the country, and the insidious practice was beginning to fade in Oklahoma as well. The issues of segregation and disproportionate legislative representation would help lead to closer federal oversight of Oklahoma's political climate.

Framework of the Court System

Consistent with early-twentieth-century southern political practice, the authors of the state's constitution structured the courts in a way designed to minimize the expenditure of tax dollars. This was especially true at the level closest to the average citizen: the trial judges. The state government had three levels of trial judges: district judges, county judges, and justices of the peace (JPs). The JPs were the lowest rung of the judicial ladder and became the most controversial part of the trial court system.

JPs were hardly unique to Oklahoma. The office of justice of the peace had been established in fourteenth-century England and was an important part of the English legal structure. Although the higher-ranking assize judges in Elizabethan and Stuart England sometimes questioned the competence, integrity, and work ethic of the JPs, they performed the necessary, day-to-day, routine work of the courts. This allowed the assize judges, who traveled a circuit and were therefore not routinely present, time to hear the more important cases.[11]

Britain's American colonies inherited the JP system, which initially worked well enough that into the early twentieth century every state had adopted some form of that system. In a world where travel was limited and hazardous and communication primitive and slow, the office of justice of the peace provided a low-cost and quick method of settling minor disputes and keeping the public peace. A capable justice of the peace, regardless of his lack of legal training, could use common sense and good judgment to keep and restore order in the community, especially in rural areas without ready access to more sophisticated courts. When Oklahoma became a state in 1907, the drafters of the state's constitution established the office without serious controversy or debate.

The JPs in Oklahoma adjudicated traffic offenses, low-level misdemeanors, the preliminary stages of felony cases, and unlike their English predecessors, very small civil suits. Despite their judicial function, JPs were not lawyers and were primarily responsible for the collection of fees. JPs received part of the fines and fees as their compensation, which meant the person deciding the guilt or innocence of the accused had a vested interest in the outcome. If the accused were found not guilty, no fine would result, and the JP would have less income. The JP, after collecting the funds, was then responsible for deducting his portion and paying the balance to the county, a system that occasionally led to embezzlement charges when the JP failed to remit the funds that were due.[12]

JPs also performed marriages. Weddings were a source of significant income, especially for JPs living in counties bordering other states. One JP in Bryan County, which borders Texas, became well-known for presiding over marriages at all times of the day and night and on every day of the year. The performance of spontaneous or short-notice weddings, even though a useful service, hardly added to the reputation of the office of justice of the peace.

One of the advantages of the JP system was in the pursuit of small debts for local businesses, which could collect unpaid accounts through the JP courts at minimal cost.[13] A legal scholar of the 1920s described this aspect of the JP's job as follows: "If the reader were to attend a session of these courts, he would probably observe the disposition of a run of cases somewhat as follows: first, there would be an attorney representing a merchant or a collection agency, who would present in rapid succession the claims of his clients for merchandise sold and delivered, and the amounts of the various claims would be $2.75, $12.50, $65.10, and $99.50. Next, there would be a landlord suing for a month's unpaid rent; then, a housewife demanding satisfaction from a cleaner for ruining her evening dress; then, the neighborhood capitalist asking for judgment on a promissory note; and finally a man demanding the value of his lawn mower from a neighbor who had borrowed it and failed to return it."[14] With the exception of the amounts of money in controversy, this procedure was similar to Oklahoma's small claims court as it exists today.

By the 1920s, serious legal scholars were questioning the desirability and credibility of the JP courts, especially the fee system.[15] The advent of the automobile and, in particular, the traffic ticket greatly diminished the office's reputation. Traffic fines and small-town speed traps often led to a hapless driver being brought before a JP, who had a financial stake in fining the driver. In the words of one historian of the office, "This practice created a public conception of the Justice of the Peace as a small-town tyrant and sharp dealer whose only purpose was to harass the motoring public, or preside over the marriage of couples eloping from jurisdictions where more stringent regulations governed entrance into the state of marital bliss."[16]

By the 1960s the existence of JPs had drawn fire nationwide, and states were beginning either to modify the office or abolish it altogether.[17] Nearly every state that still had JPs began to take a skeptical look at the office. A New York University Law School study outlined the system's shortcomings, which, according to the authors, made the system "notorious." These problems included lack of legal training, part-time or inadequate service, compensation by fee, archaic procedures, and makeshift facilities.[18]

Oklahoma's JP system contained all these deficiencies. In both 1963 and 1965 the Oklahoma House of Representatives passed legislation lowering the JP civil jurisdiction to one dollar; in both cases the Senate rejected the measure. In short, by the time the Oklahoma Supreme Court scandal was exposed, the office of JP was seen nationwide as obsolete and part of a system with dubious ability and integrity. Although justices of the peace had nothing whatsoever to do with the bribery scandal, the enactment of court reform would sweep JPs out of existence in Oklahoma.

In addition to JPs, Oklahoma's judicial framework guaranteed to each county one county judge, who usually decided probates, adoptions, juvenile cases, and other routine matters. County judges, who rarely heard hotly contested or criminal matters, were paid from county funds and were considered county employees. Often, especially in rural counties, the county judge's workload and pay were minimal.[19]

Serious disputed cases were reserved for district judges, who adjudicated felonies, large-scale civil cases, and divorces. In rural areas, district judges sat in more than one county, which meant that important judicial business often had to wait for the judge to come to town. District judges and county court clerks also set the budgets for the local courts, giving them enormous power over personnel and courthouse improvements. Neither the Supreme Court nor any other agency had oversight power over district court revenue; the local district judges and court clerks spent local funds as they saw fit.[20] While district judges received their paychecks from the Supreme Court office, they actually received part of their salary from the state and the rest from the counties they served.[21]

Each of Oklahoma's seventy-seven counties had a county attorney who was responsible for criminal prosecutions and legal advice for the county government. Low pay for county attorneys and county judges made the offices attractive primarily to young lawyers seeking to establish a community reputation or to gain courtroom experience; lawyers in mid-career simply could not afford to serve. County attorneys therefore routinely ceded courtroom experience to opposing lawyers, placing the prosecution at a disadvantage. The county attorney system was so unsatisfactory that even the Oklahoma Association of County Attorneys recommended the office's abolition, arguing that the establishment of a district attorney system would provide more efficient law enforcement, especially in rural counties.[22]

Courtrooms were busy places, but whether the litigants routinely received justice is debatable.[23] With few discovery rules, the parties learned in the courtroom itself, often for the first time, the relative strengths or weaknesses of their cases. The legal system encouraged only minimal pretrial discovery or pleadings; without meaningful discovery, many cases that should have been resolved outside the courtroom went to trial. Without adequate pretrial procedures and strong, enforceable court rules, the system was subject to manipulation by argumentative, forceful attorneys who relied as much on the strength of their own personalities as on the facts and the law. Trials often became a spectator sport more notable for their entertainment value and surprise tactics than the achievement of justice.

Unlike most states, Oklahoma had two appellate courts of last resort: the Court of Criminal Appeals, which heard only criminal cases, and the Supreme Court, which heard all other appeals as well as lawyer licensing issues. The Court of Criminal Appeals, until 1959 unfortunately named the Criminal Court of Appeals, was created by the first legislature. Its three members, expanded to five in 1988, served from three nominating districts.[24]

The Supreme Court consisted of nine justices, each elected from a geographically designated district.[25] No intermediate appellate courts existed, so every noncriminal appeal—regardless of importance, merit, legal complexity, or case size—went to the Supreme Court. Even with the Court of Criminal Appeals hearing criminal cases, this created a high workload for the Supreme Court.[26] Except for the extremely rare case involving interpretation of the U.S. Constitution, the decision of the Supreme Court (or the Court of Criminal Appeals in criminal cases) was final; a party losing its case at that level had nowhere else to go. The final winners and losers of civil litigation in Oklahoma were therefore determined by the Supreme Court. The Supreme Court and the Court of Criminal Appeals both also set precedent; their published decisions were binding authority for lower courts.

Justices and judges were elected officials, answerable only to the will of the voters.[27] Appellate justices and judges ran from specific nominating districts as representatives of the Democratic or Republican Parties. Since they were secondary officials on long ballots in issueless races, the job tenure of judges depended to a great extent on political affiliation. Usually, although not always, the Democratic nominee won. In 1928, however, Al Smith's unpopularity doomed many Democratic judges to defeat, even though they had nothing to do with the presidential candidate. In the 1930s the strength of Franklin D. Roosevelt's candidacy swept Democratic judges back into office, even though they likewise had no affiliation with the New Deal.

The nominating district was a very peculiar political creation.[28] A Supreme Court justice or Court of Criminal Appeals judge ran for his party's nomination from his own geographic district, based on the candidate's residence. The party's nominees were then subject to a statewide general election. A party's judicial candidate nominated by voters of his party from a district in northeast Oklahoma, for example, ran in the general election as a statewide candidate, not just from northeast Oklahoma. Every voter in the state was eligible to cast a vote not only for the judicial candidate from the voter's own district but for all districts that were on the ballot. This practice clearly benefited the majority party.

Justice N. S. Corn almost certainly benefited from the existence of the nominating district. Corn, a Democrat, came from Republican-oriented northwest Oklahoma. In 1934, as Democratic a year as can be imagined in Oklahoma, Corn ran for his district's Supreme Court seat. He obtained the nomination and was elected in the statewide election, unseating the Republican incumbent. Corn then was reelected, still as a Democrat in a Republican-leaning district, in statewide elections in 1940, 1946, and 1952.

Since judges were partisan elected officials, they felt comfortable and, in some cases, obliged to make partisan political speeches and endorse other candidates. A judicial candidate had the possibility of facing the electorate in three elections: the primary, the runoff, and the general election. Some judges campaigned for nonjudicial office without leaving the bench. A judge, therefore, not only represented the judicial system; he also represented his political party.[29]

The experience of Justice Harry Halley illustrates this point. In 1946 Halley, a Democrat, occupied the post of district judge in Tulsa County. In the election that postwar year, Tulsa County voters swept all Republican candidates into office, and Halley lost his post. Two years later, in 1948, Halley was elected as a Democrat to the Supreme Court, where he served until 1967. Because of his political affiliation, Halley had therefore been turned out of his job as district judge only to have that same affiliation lead to his promotion to the Supreme Court in the next election. Justice Halley, who became a strong proponent of court reform, later drily remarked on the irony of his apparent improvement as a judge in his two years out of office.[30]

The ballot box constituted the only means for the public to express approval or disapproval of judicial performance. Other than the cumbersome and impractical legislative impeachment process, no mechanism existed for removing corrupt, incompetent, or infirm judges. Judicial retirement plans did not exist, so once a judge left office, his income stopped. Judges therefore had every incentive to hang onto their jobs as long as they could.

Distrust of the Court

By the late 1950s the Oklahoma Supreme Court had become a place of public suspicion. Members of the legal community and of the general public, then and now, have a natural, innate reluctance to speak badly of the courts. Despite this, in his successful 1958 campaign for a seat on the court, William A. Berry constantly ran into voters and officials who expressed distrust of the Supreme Court. One of his personal friends, whose father had been a successful highway contractor, worried about Berry's becoming contaminated by the "crooks on that thing." Among lawyers, *In Re Meadors Estate*, a highly publicized will contest in which the justices had reversed their own ruling, created considerable controversy and was the source of rumors of misconduct.

Other unprofessional practices harmed the credibility of the Oklahoma judicial system as a whole. Tolerance of allowing ex parte communications between judges and attorneys, hardly limited to the Supreme Court, also contributed to the general distrust of the system. At the time of the scandal, Oklahoma had been a state for only two generations, and it still retained much of its rural, informal flavor. Lawyers would commonly drop by a judge's chambers to discuss a case with him; many lawyers considered this to be good legal practice, not unethical or inappropriate behavior. Judges had limited support staffs, and stopping in to see the judge was a simple affair.[31] Although these practices were common knowledge in the legal community, lawyers were reluctant to complain. Since no mechanism existed for investigating or removing a judge, any complaint would have been futile; nobody had the authority to receive or investigate a complaint, much less act on it.

The judicial habit of allowing ex parte discussion of cases gave an advantage to lawyers who violated the rules. Justice Berry wrote that the practice had become so accepted that lawyers came to expect it and were surprised if judges refused to participate. Lawyers who played by the rules ran a risk; if the lawyer failed to discuss the case with the judge outside the courtroom, the other side might have done so and defeated him before the trial even began. Litigants also had a choice to make. If they did not hire a lawyer with political connections, the other side might. Litigation therefore often became a race to the politically connected lawyer's office.

In 1951, students of the University of Oklahoma's law review studied Oklahoma's court practices and compared them to the minimum standards suggested by the American Bar Association's Judicial Administration Section. With one exception—the fair selection of jurors—Oklahoma's judicial system failed all the standards. Oklahoma's practices of judicial selection, judicial partisanship, the judiciary's lack of organization and supervision, its failure to keep meaningful statistics, the lack of a judicial retirement system, the existence of justice of the peace courts, and the lack of meaningful pretrial conferences all fell woefully short of ABA recommendations.[32]

Scandals can occur in nearly any political system. However, the weaknesses of Oklahoma's political and judicial structures helped create an environment in which corruption became nearly inevitable and made exposure and prosecuting for misconduct exceedingly difficult. The details and personalities of the scandal should cause observers to reflect back on what Oklahoma politics owed to its southern influences, which featured an ironclad resistance to change, and the state's unfortunate tendency to look the other way while important decisions are being made behind closed doors, without public knowledge or input.

Selected Investments

One of the most important factors in studying Oklahoma's judicial scandal is an understanding of the deep-seated relationship between powerful private interests and public figures. The largest and most notorious example of this in Oklahoma is Selected Investments (Selected), a company formed in 1929 by Hugh A. Carroll, a businessman and former schoolteacher from northwestern Oklahoma. For the most part, Selected Investments began with small consumer loans; its advertisements during the 1930s urged customers to "borrow to save money" and advertised loans "from $50 to $350" at the company's office in downtown Oklahoma City. Selected Investments routinely lent money for the purchase of "diamonds, cars, furniture, or other personal property" and asked its customers to "get rid of money worries—use our loan plan."[33]

By the 1940s, Selected Investments had become wildly profitable and begun to diversify. Taking advantage of the Roosevelt-era programs of Veterans Administration and Federal Housing Administration financing, Selected opened a real estate office in growing northwest Oklahoma City, selling and renting "good homes, all northwest."[34] In 1948 the company opened a new headquarters across the street from the Oklahoma County courthouse, inviting potential investors to visit.

While Selected Investments heavily advertised its small loan and real estate businesses, the company's most profitable and controversial enterprise involved its investment bond program for small investors. Charging a 2-percent-per-year management fee, the company's offer to potential investors was simple: Selected Investments guaranteed a 6 percent per year return on the investment. Regardless of war, depression, market variances, or other economic calamity, a participant who invested ten thousand dollars was guaranteed an annual dividend of six hundred dollars, plus immediate return of the full investment on demand.

In hindsight, the idea that an investment company could offer guaranteed profits at no risk to the customer seems preposterous, and it is easy to wonder why anyone could fall for such a proposal. However, a reading of Selected's advertising helps explain the company's appeal. As its advertisements pointed out, by 1947 Selected had delivered on its promises for seventeen years without any investor losing a penny. Selected falsely claimed that all funds were held in trust, that they were subject to regular audits by public accountants, and that all their bonds were collateralized. The company emphasized the security of the investment, claiming, "It's safe—it's cashable—it earns 6%."[35]

However, not everyone was enamored with Selected Investments. Under Oklahoma's system, securities were regulated by the office of the bank commissioners, which in 1950 had only two investigators to cover the entire state. One of those investigators was Herschal K. Ross, a former Greer County court clerk who had been employed by the banking commissioner for only a few months and lacked regulatory experience. Ross would later become entangled in the affairs of Selected Investments. The other investigator, unfortunately for Selected Investments, was Milton B. Cope, a stubborn and persistent lawyer who had worked at the agency for several years and was, according to his boss, an "experienced analyst of values of securities."[36] Cope intensely distrusted Selected Investments and, to the extent of his limited resources, made it his mission to get to the bottom of the company's financial affairs.

In February 1950 the banking commissioner, at Cope's urging, suspended Selected Investment's authority to sell securities. Selected, represented by State Senator James Rinehart, immediately went to the Oklahoma County district court and obtained a temporary restraining order preventing the commissioner from acting. For a year the case simply sat dormant with the restraining order in place. Selected Investments retained its ability to sell securities, but the company's position remained precarious.

One of the candidates to succeed outgoing governor Roy Turner was Johnston Murray, the son of Oklahoma's eccentric and controversial former governor William H. "Alfalfa Bill" Murray, a man whose style and politics symbolized southern political culture in Oklahoma. Alfalfa Bill Murray had chaired the Oklahoma constitutional convention, served as the first Speaker of the Oklahoma House of Representatives, served in Congress during the Woodrow Wilson administration, founded a failed colony in Bolivia, and become a folksy national figure during a term as governor during the Great Depression. With his appeal to rural white voters, his odd mannerisms, his unpredictable and volatile behavior, and his hatred for big business, Alfalfa Bill became the best-known Oklahoma political figure of his time.[37]

Alfalfa Bill's son, Johnston, took a circuitous route to the 1950 governor's race. After he graduated from what was then known as the Murray School of Agriculture (named after his father and now Murray State College), Johnston and his family joined his father's colonial expedition in Bolivia. After the colony failed, Johnston returned to Oklahoma and pursued business ventures in newspapers, cattle, and oil. In 1946 the forty-three-year-old Murray graduated from the Oklahoma City University School of Law.[38] Four years later, with no political experience, he entered the field as a candidate for governor.

Although Murray began his campaign as a dark horse, he captured the voting public's imagination as the son of Alfalfa Bill and as "just plain folks." As also occurred in other southern and borderland states, Murray's campaign drew strength from conservatives, anti–New Deal Democrats, and antialcohol dry forces.[39] After a bitter and ugly runoff, Murray won the Democratic nomination and then narrowly defeated his Republican opponent in the general election.[40]

Murray's campaign had needed money, and Selected Investments, under attack from the banking commissioner, had helped provide it. In exchange for Murray's promise to get rid of Milton B. Cope, Hugh Carroll put "four figures" into Murray's campaign through William Doenges, a Bartlesville auto dealer and former Democratic national committeeman.⁴¹ Once in office, Murray did not directly fire Cope; instead, that spring, Senator George Miskovsky of Oklahoma City, who was also an attorney for Selected Investments, introduced a bill establishing the Oklahoma Securities Commission and stripping the banking commissioner of his securities regulation responsibilities.⁴² Carroll, a private citizen given the chance to address the legislative committee considering the bill, argued that Cope was a director in a building and loan company and was therefore prejudiced against Carroll. The solution, therefore, according to Carroll and his supporters, was to legislate Cope out of state government.⁴³ Miskovsky, who had senatorial privilege over appointments in his Oklahoma County district, increased the pressure by refusing to move the nomination of O. B. Mothersead, Cope's boss, as head of the state banking department.⁴⁴ Senator James Rinehart, Selected's lawyer in the litigation with the banking department, continued to back the bill eliminating Cope's job, which of course would end the lawsuit in Rinehart's client's favor. Dissenters pointed out the troublesome promises made in Selected's advertising, with one representative comparing the literature to an advertisement for patent medicine and arguing, "No banking institution in the world can pay six percent as advertised here. . . . This company could go busted." Senator Roy Grantham, later the presiding officer in N. B. Johnson's impeachment trial, prophetically warned that passage of the bill would "return to haunt the senators in a decade."⁴⁵

The securities bill became the last legislation considered by the 1951 legislature, and it was the object of bitter debate. For unclear reasons, Miskovsky suddenly withdrew from the discussion and unsuccessfully moved to kill his own bill. Governor Murray publicly took a hands-off approach but strongly supported the bill behind the scenes. Although Doenges denied sponsoring the bill, he and Carroll were seen together in Murray's office after the bill passed. Led by Representatives J. D. McCarty and Paul Harkey in the House and Rinehart, who represented Selected Investments in the conflict with the banking commissioner, in the Senate, the bill passed both houses in the legislature's last act before adjourning. Cope was out of a job, and the investigation of Selected Investments died on the vine.⁴⁶ Herschal Ross assumed Cope's duties; within a few years, Ross's son was an employee of Selected Investments, an entity his father regulated.

Selected Investments had successfully thrown its money around. By buying influence with the governor and employing lawyer-legislators to represent the company, Selected had used the power of the legislature and governor to end a governmental investigation into its finances.[47] Very few people had thought to ask the appropriate questions: How was the company paying a guaranteed 6 percent return, and had Cope correctly smelled a rat? Selected continued to do business as usual, expanding into real estate and other areas, creating so many subsidiary corporations that eventually even Carroll could not keep track of them.[48] The company's corporate interests included ventures in real estate, mortgage lending, apartments, home furnishings, automobiles, publishing, variety stores, farm stores, a dairy, and a factory.[49] By the time of its fall, Selected Investments had about ten thousand investors, most of them Oklahomans, with a company-claimed value of about $40 million. About one thousand of those investors came from Oklahoma City.[50]

O. A. Cargill

O. A. Cargill was born in 1885 in northern Arkansas and spent his early years living the challenging life of a child of a subsistence farmer.[51] When he was sixteen, Cargill left Arkansas for Stroud, Indian Territory.[52] A huge and physically imposing young man, Cargill worked variously as a muleskinner, ranch hand, and storekeeper for a general store that catered almost exclusively to members of the Sac and Fox tribe. He also became a justice of the peace, which made him interested in the study of law. He and his wife moved to Oklahoma City, where he worked as a streetcar conductor and police officer until he passed the bar in 1916. Sixteen months after he became a lawyer, Cargill was appointed Oklahoma County attorney.

While Cargill served as Oklahoma County's chief prosecutor, he participated in a horrific lynching. In August 1920, two Oklahoma County police officers, who were outside of their jurisdiction, and the owner of a whiskey still were killed in a gun battle in neighboring Logan County. The still owner's son, a young African American man named Claude Chandler, was arrested for the murder of the officers. Although his office had no jurisdiction over homicides that occurred in another county, Cargill, claiming the Logan County officials were treating the bodies of the deceased officers inappropriately, forcibly seized control of the scene, probably at gunpoint.[53] Cargill allegedly claimed that a jury composed of Logan County residents, which had a higher percentage of African Americans than Oklahoma County, would have acquitted Chandler. He then ordered Chandler placed in the Oklahoma County jail, even though the crime had occurred elsewhere.

That night Claude Chandler was forcibly taken from the Oklahoma County jail and lynched. The jailer claimed to have been overpowered by three armed, unidentified men after the employee had mistakenly unlocked the outside door. A modern-day journalist who has studied the Chandler lynching concluded that the person who removed Chandler from the jail was actually a deputy sheriff, and that Ned Looney, then an assistant county attorney and later to be Cargill's lifelong friend, colleague, and sometime rival, provided the deputy with a phony alibi. After Chandler's disappearance from the jail, someone entered the words "Nigger lost" on the jail log.[54] The journalist also located a macabre postcard photo of the lynching; the card was signed by a person named Ned.

Cargill's tenure as county attorney coincided with a terrible time for race relations in Oklahoma. In the 1920s the Ku Klux Klan was one of the leading political voices in the state; the organization had an enormous influence on the legislature and the governor's office. Vigilante justice occurred frequently; the day before Chandler's murder, a white man accused of killing a cab driver had been lynched in Tulsa. The next year saw the horrendous Tulsa Race Massacre, which killed at least seventy-nine people, most of them African Americans, and destroyed the thriving African American Greenwood neighborhood in the city.[55] In Claude Chandler's case, no one was ever brought to justice for his death. Chandler's death was an awful episode in an ugly time; the evidence shows that Cargill enabled and encouraged the lynching.

In 1923 Cargill was elected mayor of Oklahoma City. Three years later he entered the race for the Democratic nomination for governor. Although his gubernatorial campaign began well, Cargill alienated voters with his heavy-handed personal style and his flip-flopping on issues, especially on the subject of the Klan. He finished a poor third in the Democratic primary, ending his political career.[56]

Cargill became an extremely successful and wealthy attorney, handling important and highly publicized civil and criminal litigation. He retained his reputation for bombastic behavior in the courtroom, once earning himself a one-day jail sentence from his future ally Judge Ben Arnold. He purchased a large ranch north of Oklahoma City, which he enjoyed with his family. The ranch produced oil, from which he acquired a substantial income.

Although he was extremely successful financially, his standing among his peers was shaky. Cargill's reputation took a serious blow in 1939, when he accused a shadowy acquaintance, Roy Alford, of using a false name to break into Cargill's safety deposit box and steal five thousand dollars. Alford testified at trial that Cargill claimed to have bribed two of the three members of the Criminal Court of Appeals to hold the state's liquor permit law unconstitutional. Alford also claimed to have copies of checks implying Cargill had bribed five Oklahoma City councilmen to approve settlement of a pollution case. Although Alford was acquitted, he obviously was not very credible, and no investigation ensued. However, the prosecutor and the judge both indicated they agreed with the jury's verdict, which showed that neither of them believed Cargill's testimony.[57] They did not know that by the time of this incident, Cargill had already developed an illegal financial relationship with Justice N. S. Corn of the Oklahoma Supreme Court. Although Cargill was capable of considerable generosity, especially with his church, his behavior throughout his life consistently demonstrated enormous ambition, a disregard for rules, and the willingness to overpower other people in order to win.

N. S. Corn

Like Cargill, Nelson Smith Corn was a product of the frontier. In 1894, when Corn was ten years old, his family moved to Taloga in what is now Dewey County, a place that at that time had been open to white settlement for only about ten years.[58] Corn taught school for a few years before being elected Dewey County clerk in 1922.[59] Corn wanted to become a lawyer, and through the use of borrowed books and an extension course he passed the bar examination, a common method of becoming a lawyer at the time. In 1926 he became the Dewey County attorney, an experience that did not go well. Soon thereafter Corn resigned and entered private practice in Taloga.[60]

In 1934 Corn announced his candidacy for the Democratic nomination for the Oklahoma Supreme Court from the state's fourth district. State law allowed each party to nominate a candidate for each of the nine Supreme Court seats, which were divided into geographic districts. The candidate was required to live in that district. Voters from the entire state then voted on the nominees in the general election. Justices were elected for six-year terms, with the terms staggered so that three seats were open each election.

Corn's qualifications for the job were questionable. Although he was fifty years old, he had been a lawyer for only about eight years, and he had never been a judge. His experience as a public official included only short stints as Dewey County clerk and Dewey County attorney. Nonetheless, Corn won the Democratic nomination in a runoff.[61] In the general election, Corn faced

Republican incumbent Charles Swindall, who had defeated the Democratic incumbent six years earlier in the backlash to the unpopular presidential candidacy of Al Smith.[62] The Supreme Court race drew little public interest and had no legal or political issues. This did not matter; in 1934 the Democrats won every single statewide race, including Corn's.[63] Corn, coming from Republican-leaning northwestern Oklahoma, without a doubt benefited from the fact that Supreme Court races were determined by a statewide vote in the general election. The Great Depression, so terrible for so many, had provided the opportunity of a lifetime for Corn.

A year after he assumed the bench, Justice Corn and O. A. Cargill began a relationship based on corruption. As Corn later testified, Cargill called Justice Corn and asked him to come to Cargill's law office in downtown Oklahoma City. At the meeting Cargill told Corn he wanted to win his appellate cases by a "fair margin" and wanted Corn to act as the sixth vote on opinions. From that point on, according to Corn, Cargill routinely called Justice Corn and told him to "get your pencil out." He then told Corn what case he was calling about and then told him to "follow the crowd." In the early years, Cargill routinely gave Corn one thousand dollars, especially at campaign time; Corn later estimated the total amount he received early in the relationship to be about forty-five hundred dollars.[64] In one case, *American Savings Life v. Loomis*, Cargill remarkably called Corn and instructed him to vote against Cargill's position. According to Corn, Cargill explained that he had an agreement with the lawyers for the opposing side for the opponents to win.[65]

Corn's shocking testimony about his experience with Cargill raises questions that will almost certainly never be answered. Why would Cargill call Corn, whom he apparently did not know well, and demand that he come to his office to discuss bribery? When he needed only five votes out of nine, why would Cargill risk exposure and imprisonment to get a sixth? Why would Cargill spend money just to get an unnecessary sixth vote? On the cases in which he only wanted a sixth vote, how did he know he already had five? How did Cargill know when the court would hear cases and to whom they were assigned? The conclusion is inescapable that Cargill had sources other than Corn inside the court.

In the 1940s, in addition to his work as a justice on the Oklahoma Supreme Court, Corn also operated short-term small loan companies, similar to those run by Selected Investments. These businesses charged what Corn himself later termed "usurious interest." Corn did not publicly disclose his interest in these businesses, the propriety of which was very questionable for a full-time judge.[66] Corn also seemed to have considerably more cash than appropriate for a salaried state employee. From World War II until the banker changed jobs in 1952, Corn's banker broke large bills for Corn as often as three or four times per month; the source of the money is unclear.[67]

Corn successfully ran for reelection in 1940 and 1946, easily defeating Republican opponents in the overwhelmingly Democratic general elections. In 1952 he survived a scare in the Democratic primary, in which two of his colleagues were unseated, before beating his Republican opponent. Despite his having won four statewide elections, Corn's work ethic was questionable. After the exposure of the scandal, Corn's former judicial colleagues discussed his office habits. According to them, Corn "never worked and appeared never to know where he was headed." This is consistent with his later testimony to authorities; Justice Corn, despite more than two decades on the state's highest court, seemed to have only vague concepts of legal issues and little curiosity about the cases he was deciding.[68]

In April 1957 N. S. Corn announced his decision to retire from the court. He had health problems; in early 1957 he underwent surgery for colon cancer and had spent three weeks in the hospital, then a substantial period of time recovering at home.[69] At age seventy-three, he faced a reelection fight the next year against a younger candidate. A DUI arrest and other negative publicity he had received over the years were problematic. His re-election campaign would have been grueling, with a very good chance Corn would lose.

Corn's decision not to run was made easier by a recent change to the law. Until the previous year, a retiring or defeated judge, regardless of age or years of service, was simply out of a job and therefore without income. In 1956, however, at Justice Earl Welch's urging, the legislature created a position called "supernumerary judge," in which a retired judge could accept a reduced salary and an office in return for part-time service. The supernumerary position was available only to judges who voluntarily retired from office, not to those who had been defeated for reelection. Had Corn lost his reelection bid in 1958, he therefore would not have been eligible for supernumerary status.[70] Corn accepted the supernumerary position, and his term expired in January 1959. So far as the public knew, Corn had ended a long, if unspectacular, career as a jurist. His involvement with Selected Investments, which had suffered a very public fall the previous year, went temporarily unexposed.

For the six decades after statehood, Oklahoma's legal system had failed to progress. Although the office of JP had long since become obsolete, the state continued to employ JPs, whose fee system and lack of professionalism created a black eye for the entire judiciary. Poor pay for county judges and county attorneys led to constant turnover for a job with little appeal for experienced lawyers. The system of down-ballot election of justices and judges provided little or no accountability, making a seat on the bench just another political position, in which the judge owed his loyalty to the political party and campaign supporters. The lines between routine legal behavior and favoritism became blurred. This made the state ripe for corruption and its legal system easily exploited by men like Cargill and Corn.

The conservative nature of Oklahoma's officeholders and electorate made reform difficult. As I show in later chapters, even after it became obvious that Oklahoma's court system had serious flaws, efforts at reform repeatedly failed, despite the fact that the proposals were hardly drastic. Eventually both parties were to provide united leadership, which would lead the electorate, however grudgingly and hesitantly, to approve needed, meaningful improvements to the state's judicial framework.

❖ 2
The State of the Court

By the 1950s the Oklahoma Supreme Court had become a center of institutionalized corruption. The state's legal community widely believed that favorable rulings went not to the litigant with the better case but rather to the one with the better connections. Most, but by no means all, of the rumors involved Corn and Cargill in some respect. The common thread of the cases was not simply the identity of the actors; instead, it was the general atmosphere of illicit, backdoor influence on the court by lawyers willing to pay for inappropriate access and judges willing to sell it.

In 1954 the Supreme Court decided *Johnson v. Johnson*, a will contest involving the large estate of Oklahoma City attorney Dexter G. Johnson.[1] Johnson left a sheet of paper, partly typed and partly in his own handwriting, in which he had purportedly disinherited his brother. Oklahoma law interprets wills strictly. Typewritten wills must be signed and dated in front of witnesses; holographic (handwritten) wills, must be entirely in the hand of the person writing the will and must be dated and signed. Johnson's will did not meet either requirement, and the Oklahoma court probate judge denied its admission to probate.

The Supreme Court unanimously affirmed the trial court's decision and denied a petition for additional review. However, in February 1954, after the time for rehearing should have expired and the case been made final, Justice Ben Arnold presented a substitute opinion reversing the trial court and admitting the will to probate. Three months later Fred Suits, the attorney representing the family members opposing the will, received a disturbing call from Justice Harry Halley. Halley told Suits that he would lose the case, explaining that O. A. Cargill, who had not previously been involved in the Johnson matter, had been "hanging around" Arnold's office on most mornings. On October 15 a substitute opinion admitting Johnson's will, approved by Arnold, Corn, Welch, and Johnson was released. On the same day, Arnold, accompanied by his friend O. A. Cargill, purchased a new Cadillac at an Oklahoma City dealership.[2] That same week Corn also bought a used Cadillac at a dealership in Coffeyville, Kansas.³ Only one thing had changed from the time of the opinion denying the admission of the will to the release of the revised opinion admitting it eight months later: the undisclosed, private involvement of O. A. Cargill.

An earlier example of Cargill's business practices had occurred in 1948. Laura Fleming and her husband had become involved in a dispute over an oil and gas lease with D. L. Kelly, who claimed to be a silent partner of Cargill's on the lease. The Flemings lost their case at trial. After the decision, Kelly approached the Flemings, telling them that Cargill, who had not participated as an attorney in the case, wanted to speak with them without their lawyer being present. When they attended the meeting alone, Cargill told the Flemings he had "fixed" the district judge and also had the supreme court fixed. Cargill offered the Flemings twelve hundred dollars for their lease. The Flemings filed an affidavit detailing the conversation with Cargill, then repudiated their own affidavit. After they repudiated their story, Cargill paid the Flemings four thousand dollars for their lease, then drilled two oil wells on the land.⁴

Cargill was by no means the only influence-peddler at the Supreme Court. Oklahoma City attorney Wayne Bayless, a former justice who had been defeated for reelection in 1948 by N. B. Johnson, also took advantage of opportunities to make money by buying judicial votes. In 1953 Bayless and Tulsa attorney John Wheeler approached Font Allen, a Tulsa lawyer representing a plaintiff in a medical negligence case.⁵ Bayless and Wheeler told Allen that he and his client needed help with Justices Corn and Arnold. After the case was affirmed and the defendant paid the seventy-three-thousand-dollar judgment, Bayless and Wheeler demanded ten thousand dollars from Allen, which Allen paid with five-hundred-dollar bills.⁶ In another instance five years later, Bayless paid Cargill ten thousand dollars for a favorable result in an oil and gas case, which Cargill apparently split with Oklahoma City attorney Ned Looney.⁷

In 1955 the court considered the confusing Meadors will case, officially styled *Battle v. Mason*.⁸ In the 1890s, C.F. Meadors, a father of two young daughters, divorced in Arkansas. Meadors later moved to Oklahoma, remarried, and became wealthy. In 1950, while in failing health, Meadors signed a will which left $75,000 to each of his daughters, but left most of his estate to his brothers and sister. The issue before the court was whether Meadors was competent at the time he signed the will. Ned Looney's firm, which had a close relationship with Justice Welch, represented the Meadors brothers and sisters, while Cargill represented the Meadors daughters.[9] At trial Oklahoma City district judge W. A. "Lon" Carlile, later to be on the Supreme Court himself, ruled Meadors had been incompetent and refused to admit the will. Looney appealed.

As it had the previous year on the Johnson will case, the court made a fool of itself. Early in 1955 the justices issued an opinion affirming the trial court. Later that year, however, the court reconsidered. In the meantime, two new justices, including Justice Floyd Jackson, joined the court. Cargill drove to Purcell to visit Jim Nance, a newspaper publisher and state legislator, and offered Nance ten thousand dollars for Jackson's vote. Nance declined, but for some reason did not tell Jackson or anyone else about the conversation for several years.[10] Ten years after the case was decided, Justice Ben T. Williams testified that an unnamed person had offered his father, a Stratford mail carrier, a twenty-five-thousand-dollar "campaign contribution" for Williams's vote.

Williams and Justice Harry Halley both noticed an inordinate interest in the case from both Corn and Justice Ben Arnold.[11] Arnold and Corn became involved in a physical altercation during a Supreme Court conference, an extraordinary and sadly comical event that became well-known at the capitol.[12] Arnold complained that someone was "trying to do something to a friend [Cargill]." In the event, Jackson's swing vote changed the result, and to considerable public disgust the court reversed its own ruling. Cargill got the votes of Corn, Welch, and Johnson, but lost the case to Looney.[13]

Marshall v. Amos and the Westcotts

At approximately the same time, the court was considering *Marshall v. Amos*, a Cleveland County case that involved eight producing oil wells worth several million dollars. H. G. Marshall, an unsavory Nocona, Texas, oil promoter, had lost his case in the trial court. Through Cargill's daughter and son-in-law, Marshall had been casually acquainted with Cargill, who convinced Marshall he needed "insurance" with the Supreme Court.[14] Through Titus Haffa, a Chicago oilman who was Marshall's financial backer, Marshall and Cargill arranged a thirty-thousand-dollar fee for Cargill, payable to Cargill only upon reversal by the Supreme Court. On April 20, 1956, Haffa wrote a letter to Cargill confirming the arrangement, a strange thing to do considering the transaction's illegality. On July 13 Haffa wrote a second letter stating the thirty thousand dollars was to be paid in cash.[15] Cargill's interest in *Marshall v. Amos* was not disclosed; he made no court appearance, nor did he write a brief or do any other legitimate legal work.

Cargill called Corn at his office and told the justice he had twenty-five thousand dollars to be divided six ways if Corn would vote for an opinion reversing the trial court. Cargill told Corn he already had the votes of "the two Indians" (Welch and Johnson), Davison, Halley, and Blackbird. According to Corn, Cargill claimed he had an attorney from Tulsa taking care of Halley, a lawyer from Bristow for Blackbird, and that Cargill himself would handle Davison, Welch, and Johnson.[16] If Cargill indeed made this statement to Corn, he was lying; no credible misconduct claims were ever raised against Justices Blackbird, Halley, and Davison. On June 5, 1956, the court issued its opinion reversing the trial court and awarding the oil and gas interests to Marshall.[17] Despite the plan to pay Cargill in cash, he received a thirty-thousand-dollar cashier's check for obtaining the decision. In an apparent clumsy attempt to launder the money, he gave Wayne Bayless, the former justice, a check for twenty-five thousand dollars, who deposited the money in his own account. The next day Bayless withdrew five thousand dollars in cash and gave the cash to Cargill, who in turn paid four thousand dollars to Corn.[18]

Shortly after the release of the opinion in *Marshall v. Amos*, Harlan Grimes, a lawyer who had not been involved in the case to that point, published a pamphlet claiming that Cargill and Marshall had conspired to bribe various members of the court.[19] In 1959 Grimes filed a $5 million federal court suit on behalf of Amos, alleging Haffa and Marshall had paid Cargill thirty thousand dollars for the bribery. Cargill responded by calling the case an "unfortunate joke," adding that he hoped the court would not get any unfavorable publicity as a result of Grimes's claims. Although his accusations later proved to be relatively accurate, Grimes had no evidence with which to support his case, and within six weeks U.S. district judge Ross Rizley dismissed it, deeming it frivolous.[20]

Within four months, Grimes found himself the subject of a highly publicized disbarment proceeding, in which the final decision on whether he would keep his law license would be made by the same Supreme Court that Grimes had accused of bribery. At first Grimes seemed to be going down fighting; he demanded a public hearing and vowed to resist disbarment. However, he apparently changed his mind; on August 1, 1959, he failed to appear at his disbarment hearing and offered his resignation by phone. On March 8, 1960, the Supreme Court, disregarding the proffered resignation, disbarred

Grimes, citing his history of "evil and ungrounded attacks" on judges and lawyers.[21]

In 1958 Cargill also became involved in an appeal involving his daughter Otha Wescott and her husband, Harold. The Westcotts owned Oklahoma Company, an oil company through which Harold had allegedly defrauded his investors by overcharging for drilling and leasing expenses. The credibility of the company and its officers deteriorated so badly that a Washington County judge appointed a receiver to take over its management. Florida law enforcement authorities were also investigating the company's business practices.

Cargill intervened, once again calling Corn and offering him seventy-five hundred dollars for a reversal of the Washington County judge's order. Corn, in separate conversations with Welch and Johnson, agreed to buy their votes for twenty-five hundred dollars each. The embattled but indiscreet Westcott offered to sell a lucrative oil and gas lease to a family friend, explaining he needed the money to purchase votes from Justices Corn, Welch, Johnson, and Carlile.[22] On December 2, 1958, just a month before the terms of Corn and Carlile expired, the court reversed the trial judge.[23] The court's vote was five to four; the majority consisted of Corn, Welch, Carlile, Johnson, and Davison. After the ruling became final, Cargill again phoned Corn, who had moved to a supernumerary judge office in the state capitol. Corn picked up the money from Cargill and delivered twenty-five hundred dollars each to Welch and Johnson.[24]

Bribery and the *Selected Investments* Decision

Although Governor Johnston Murray had ended the banking commissioner's inquiry into the affairs of Selected Investments, the company continued to battle another state agency, the Oklahoma Tax Commission, over the corporate status of its companies. Selected claimed that the primary company consisted of two different entities: one corporation for the management of the trust and another one to manage the rest of the company and its income. The commission took a different view, contending that Selected Investments was in truth only one company. The financial stakes were enormous; a loss in the Supreme Court would cost Selected Investments about $560,000. Oklahoma County judge Albert Hunt ruled in favor of the tax commission, a result that threatened ruin for Selected.[25] The Internal Revenue Service was also watching the case; if Selected Investments lost, its chances of facing a backbreaking federal tax debt increased substantially.

Selected Investments appealed Judge Hunt's ruling to the Oklahoma Supreme Court. After the appeal was filed, Hugh Carroll, the company's founder, called Justice Corn, whom he had known from their years in Taloga, and told the justice he wanted to discuss something, a comment Corn undoubtedly took to mean his pending case. Corn and Carroll went to dinner at Glen's Hik'ry Inn, a steakhouse in northwest Oklahoma City. After dinner they returned to Corn's house and discussed Carroll's problem in Carroll's car. When Justice Corn asked Carroll how much a favorable result meant to him, Carroll told him it was worth $150,000. Privately astounded by the amount of the offer, Corn expressed interest in fixing the case, telling Carroll he would "see some of the other boys." Corn declined Carroll's offer of a down payment.[26] Corn was so staggered by the size of the offered bribe that a few days later he wrote the $150,000 figure down on a piece of paper, went to Carroll's office in downtown Oklahoma City, and showed Carroll the number. When Carroll confirmed the amount, Corn agreed to the proposal.[27]

The offer was indeed astounding; $150,000 in 1956 was equivalent to nearly $1.4 million in 2018. Corn did not tell Carroll how he proposed to accomplish the reversal, nor did Carroll ask. Corn agreed to commit this serious crime with no down payment from Carroll; both men acted entirely on faith. Corn had no way of knowing whether Carroll even had access to that amount of money. The conspirators never offered an explanation regarding why Carroll approached Corn in the first place; the public record shows that Corn and Carroll had only been casually acquainted from their mutual Taloga ties many year previously. Clearly, the word was out regarding corruption in the Supreme Court.

Having accepted Carroll's proposal, Corn visited Justice N. B. Johnson at Johnson's office in the capitol. Corn told Johnson he had known Carroll for many years, and that he could get Johnson seventy-five hundred dollars in exchange for his vote on an opinion favorable to Selected Investments. Johnson told Corn he did not know whether an opinion reversing the trial court could be written, but Johnson indicated he would go along if he could do so.[28] Corn then called on Justice Welch separately and had a similar conversation. Welch also agreed to participate in the scheme. At no time did Corn, Welch, and Johnson discuss the plan together; all of Corn's conversations were one-on-one talks with the other participants. Corn misled the other justices on the amount of money he was to get from Carroll, implying that he was to receive seventy-five hundred dollars as well.

Still unsure of how many votes he had, Corn called O. A. Cargill, who had not been involved in the *Selected Investments* case up to that point. Corn believed Cargill could influence the vote of Justice W. A. "Lon" Carlile, who had been appointed to the court's Oklahoma County seat after the deaths of Justice Ben Arnold and, shortly thereafter, Justice Albert Hunt. After Hunt's death, on Ned Looney's recommendation Governor Raymond Gary appointed Carlile to fill the vacancy.

William A. Berry, who defeated Carlile in 1958, described Justice Carlile as a "nice old man, genuine and outgoing, well-liked by everybody, but not really much of a factor on the court." According to Berry, Carlile's major weakness as a jurist was his tendency to be loyal to old friends, which colored his objectivity.[29] Cargill told Corn that Carlile would vote any way Cargill told him to vote.[30]

A few days after their conversation about Carlile's vote, Cargill phoned Justice Corn and told him Carlile would vote for reversal. Corn and Carlile never discussed Selected Investments privately. No hard evidence exists of any financial irregularity by Carlile; it is likely that Cargill duped Carlile into voting for reversal, pocketing the $2,500 for himself. Carlile apparently did not become curious why Cargill had contacted him about a case in which he was not representing anyone; Cargill certainly would not have told Carlile he was being paid by, of all people, another justice. Carlile's conduct is a textbook example of the then-common practice of judges allowing the ex parte discussion of cases pending before them. Although he violated judicial rules and behaved foolishly, it is unlikely that Carlile committed a crime. Whatever the case, Corn was now assured of four votes; on a court of nine justices, he only needed five.

Carroll and Corn had concocted a lucrative scheme. For the promise of $17,500 ($7,500 each to Johnson and Welch and $2,500 to Cargill for Carlile's vote), Corn stood to receive $150,000, a profit of $132,500. Carroll also expected a profit. Having paid Corn nothing before the court's opinion, Carroll had nothing to lose. If he lost the case, Selected Investments owed the tax commission what it had been already ordered to pay. If Selected won, Carroll had promised $150,000 to save $560,000.

Selected's appeal remained undecided for several months. Although no witness specifically said so, this time frame coincides with Corn's hospitalization and recovery from colon cancer.[31] As the chief justice, Earl Welch would have set the court's calendar.[32] It therefore seems likely that Welch held the case until Corn's return.

On March 12, 1957, the Oklahoma Supreme Court handed down its ruling on *Selected Investments v. Oklahoma Tax Commission*. The majority opinion was written by Chief Justice Earl Welch and was supported by five other justices, including Corn, Johnson, and Carlile. While the opinion is very difficult to understand, the author and the concurring justices held that Selected Investments Corporation and Selected Investments Trust Fund were separate, although closely related entities, and therefore should not be treated as one large taxpaying company.[33] The Tax Commission requested a rehearing, which was denied on April 2. Selected Investments had won.

On April 20, 1957, Corn called Hugh Carroll at his office and told him the mandate to the district court ordering the reversal was coming down. Carroll told Corn he was unprepared to pay the entire $150,000 immediately. Corn asked Carroll if he could pay $25,000, which Carroll agreed to pay from his personal account. Corn then called Johnson and Welch and asked them to remain at the capitol after working hours. Corn drove to Carroll's office; Carroll entered Corn's car, then placed $25,000 in Corn's glove compartment.[34] Corn then drove directly back to the capitol, went to Johnson's office, and handed him $7,500 in hundred-dollar bills, which Johnson counted in Corn's presence. Corn then did the same thing at Welch's office.[35]

On April 24 Carroll, without corporate authorization, borrowed $200,000 from the Selected Investments trust fund, the fund from which the company had the duty to pay investors. A vice president of the First National Bank wrote to Brinks, authorizing the company to deliver $200,000 cash to Carroll's office; Carroll signed a receipt from the Brinks driver that morning.[36] Carroll then called Corn and told him to come to his office; when Corn arrived, Carroll paid him the remaining $125,000. Carroll then used the rest of the investor money to repay himself the $25,000 he had previously paid Corn and retained $50,000 for himself.[37]

Thanks to O. A. Cargill, Corn had been illegally supplementing his income for years. However, he had never handled anything approaching this amount of money, which created a new problem. The $132,500 he cleared from the Selected Investments bribery was nearly ten times his annual salary; what could he do with the money without raising suspicion and exposing his own graft? For obvious reasons he could not pay cash for a home, a car, or other tangible personal property. Corn therefore stashed the money in all sorts of unusual places; he hid some in his locker at Lincoln Park golf course, some in filing cabinets in his home and his office, and still more in a fruit jar in his backyard.[38]

Corn squandered much of the money. He lent at least $6,000 to his son Lonnie. He went to Las Vegas, where he lost about $10,000, and to a racetrack in Phoenix. In the summer of 1957 Corn returned to Las Vegas with his family and lost about $15,000 on that trip. The next winter he went to Hot Springs, Arkansas, with $15,000 to $20,000 and lost much of that money as well.[39]

The Bankruptcy of Selected Investments

The expensive and illegal resolution of its litigation with the Oklahoma Tax Commission did not end Selected Investments' financial problems. The federal court was about to rule against the company, making it liable for substantial indebtedness to the IRS.[40] The combination of the impossible promises the company had made, the lavish lifestyles the executives maintained, and embezzlement took their toll. On December 8, 1957, only eight months after he paid the bribe money, Carroll wrote his investors a letter notifying them the company would not be able to honor its pledge of 6 percent return and proposing an unspecified "reorganization." Carroll's letter put certificate holders on the defensive, giving them until January 8 to accept or reject the company's vague plan. In the meantime the dividends were not paid, and certificate holders were in peril of losing their entire investments.[41]

Besieged by calls from panicked constituents and alarmed by Carroll's arbitrary January deadline, the Oklahoma legislature, which had previously turned a blind eye to the shortcomings of Selected Investments, sprang into action with a vengeance. On December 23, disregarding the holiday season, a hastily convened legislative committee met to discuss the problem. Although they had promised to attend the meeting, Carroll and two of the company's top executives, J. Phil Burns and Linwood Neal, did not show up. Carroll sent Paul Washington, his attorney and son-in-law, to appear in his stead, leaving the hapless Washington to try to explain the absence of the corporate officers. Washington unconvincingly told the committee the corporate officers were waiting on an audit and, of all things, processing an application with the U.S. Securities and Exchange Commission to sell securities throughout the country.

At the December 23 meeting, legislators concentrated their fire on Herschal K. Ross, the director of the Oklahoma Securities Commission and the man who had replaced Milton Cope six years previously. Under Ross's leadership the securities commission had become the epitome of a regulatory agency captured by those it was charged with regulating. Claiming lack of investigators, Ross had simply sat on his hands. Ross's son Ronald had worked for Selected's small loan department, and Carroll and Ross were social friends. Although Ross claimed his office had little authority, legislators pointed out that he had never complained to them about this problem. To make things worse, the securities commission's attorney member had resigned several years previously, but Ross had not reported this fact to Governor Gary, so the post had remained vacant.[42] Ross was on his way out, as he had obviously not done the job of protecting Oklahoma investors from unsound or unscrupulous business practices.

However, there was something disingenuous about the criticism Ross was receiving from the legislature. Ross had seen what had happened to M. B. Cope six years earlier; Cope's active and aggressive criticism of Selected Investments bought him a one-way ticket out of state government, courtesy of the legislature. On the *Selected Investments* case, Ross had done what he undoubtedly thought the legislature had expected him to do—very little.

Although its authority to issue subpoenas was questionable, the legislative committee issued orders to appear on January 2, 1958, to Carroll, corporate sales executive J. Phil Burns, trustee Linwood Neal, and corporate auditor Harold Hedges. Governor Gary appeared at the hearing, but the corporate officers did not, claiming the legislature lacked authority to issue subpoenas outside of a regular legislative session. Washington again tried to buy time, suggesting his client would give its investors more time to decide on how to vote on the company's reorganization proposal.[43] The next day, at Gary's insistence, the securities commission suspended Selected Investments' authority to sell securities.[44] Ross then issued new subpoenas for the four corporate officers to appear before his commission.[45]

With Selected's legal situation deteriorating daily, Corn had been talking separately with Cargill and Carroll. At Corn's insistence Carroll hired O. A. Cargill, whom he had never met, as the company's attorney.[46] Carroll also asked Corn to return the bribe money, presumably to help cover up the shortage to investigators. The next day Corn returned $33,000 in $100 bills, explaining to Carroll that sum was all he had left, and that he "didn't feel like calling on the others."[47]

When the securities commission hearing convened on January 7, Cargill accompanied Carroll and Linwood Neal to the hearing. Cargill told the two commissioners, one of whom was Herschal Ross, that his clients needed more time to prepare their testimony. When the commissioners refused, Cargill and his clients walked out of the hearing. At Governor Gary's insistence, the commissioners cited Carroll and Neal for contempt, an action the commission would be required to urge in Oklahoma County district court.

Cargill beat them to the punch. He walked directly to the Oklahoma Supreme Court and urged them to order the district court to give him more time. Although Cargill did not even file his appeal until after 3 p.m., Chief Justice Welch called an immediate hearing, which occurred late that afternoon. Ignoring the inconvenient fact that his client had already dishonored the shareholder certificates, Cargill told the court the commission's action would cause panic, comparing it to a run on a bank. After a short recess, the court granted Cargill ten days in which to file a brief and the opposing side five days to respond. Without any testimony, Cargill had achieved from the Supreme Court what he wanted—delay.[48]

The next day an Oklahoma City couple who were investors in the company filed a suit in Oklahoma County district court, asking the court to appoint a receiver for the company.[49] An order granting receivership would have legal significance in two ways. First, it would take control of the corporation away from Carroll, Burns, and the other top executives and replace them with someone appointed and supervised by the judge. Second, under federal bankruptcy law the appointment of a receiver constituted an act of involuntary bankruptcy. Once a receiver had been appointed, the company's creditors could force Selected Investments into federal bankruptcy, regardless of whether the corporate directors agreed with the decision. There were two advantages for creditors to be in bankruptcy court: the greater likelihood of some return on the creditors' investments under court control, and, with federal courts having priority over state courts, the ability to bypass state courts, including the Oklahoma Supreme Court. If Selected Investments went into bankruptcy, neither the district court nor the Oklahoma Supreme Court could protect the company any longer.

On January 9 an Oklahoma County judge appointed Oklahoma City attorney George Shirk as receiver for Selected Investments. Shirk's appointment infuriated the plaintiffs, as he had represented Selected at one time; the next month Shirk disclosed that Selected was also financing a proposed shopping center in which Shirk held stock. The judge appointed three additional receivers, who hired Luther Bohanon, a future federal judge, to represent them.[50]

Bohanon remained in the case throughout and proved to be a capable match for Selected Investments.

On Thursday, February 27, the other shoe dropped for Selected Investments. Six creditors filed a petition to compel the company to enter into involuntary bankruptcy. The case was assigned to U.S. district judge Stephen Chandler, who scheduled a hearing for the following Monday, leaving Selected one business day and the weekend to prepare for federal court. At the hearing on March 3, attended by numerous contentious lawyers representing angry investors, Chandler declared the companies bankrupt and appointed Oklahoma City attorney Paul Duncan as trustee of the companies. Because of federal court priority over state courts, the bankruptcy brought the state district court litigation to a halt. At the hearing, Judge Chandler expressed great concern for the investors, worrying openly about certificate holders who were "widows and orphans" and about investors who needed the money to buy food.[51]

Cargill and Carroll had excellent reason to be leery of Judge Chandler. Even in the eccentric Oklahoma legal world of the 1950s, Chandler stood out. He had been nominated to the federal bench in 1940 to fill one the three Oklahoma federal judgeships that happened to be open at the same time. The Department of Justice took exception to Chandler's nomination; he had little courtroom experience, he had a shaky reputation as a business operator, and he had settled a civil assault case leveled against him by a stenographer. When the objections to Chandler threatened the other two nominations, A. P. Murrah, who had just been promoted to the Tenth Circuit Court of Appeals, intervened and persuaded U.S. senator Elmer Thomas to consider Chandler's candidacy separately. This caused a delay of nearly two years in Chandler's confirmation and led to a bitter, lifelong feud with Murrah.[52]

By the time of the *Selected Investments* case, Judge Chandler had developed a perpetual and irrational fear for his life. He was convinced his enemies were tapping his phones, trying to poison his water carafe, or bomb his car. The only person allowed to have Chandler's personal phone number was the U.S. District Court clerk. A caller wishing to contact Chandler would call the clerk, who would then call Chandler's phone and allow the phone to ring a predetermined number of times. The clerk would then call back and tell Chandler who was calling, and Chandler would return the call.[53] In later years Chandler would bar the U.S. attorney and his assistants from practicing in the Western District, have his caseload temporarily removed by the Tenth

Circuit, and be unsuccessfully prosecuted for conspiring to build a private road with public funds for a subdivision he was building. The highest levels of the federal government were aware of Chandler's behavior; the U.S. Supreme Court considered and overturned his suspension by the Tenth Circuit, and his feuds with his fellow judges brought investigation by the U.S. House Judiciary Committee.[54]

After the exposure of the Supreme Court scandal, Chandler became convinced that W. H. (Pat) O'Bryan, one of Selected Investments' attorneys, had tried to perpetrate a fraud on the court by submitting a claim in excess of $1 million for services rendered. Chandler denied the claim, disbarred O'Bryan from practicing in the Western District of Oklahoma, and began a campaign to persuade prosecutors to indict O'Bryan. In August 1965 Chandler, a sitting federal judge, inaccurately and inappropriately told a newspaper that O'Bryan was "an accomplice if not the mastermind" of the Selected Investments bribery. O'Bryan retaliated with a libel suit against Chandler, which resulted in a judgment in favor of O'Bryan. The parties battled each other in a succession of federal and state appellate courts for years, until the Tenth Circuit eventually ruled in Chandler's favor.[55]

Cargill and Carroll now had serious problems. The company was in bankruptcy court with an unpredictable, volatile, and vindictive judge who had already publicly expressed his disdain for them. Bad news kept coming. On March 7, at trustee Paul Duncan's request, Chandler froze all the assets of the corporate officers, including Hugh and Julia Carroll, and ordered them into a hearing on March 17. Duncan also fired all the corporate officers.[56]

Over the weekend prior to the March 17 hearing, Hugh and Julia Carroll went to Cargill's ranch north of Oklahoma City to discuss the case.[57] Carroll told Cargill about the $150,000 bribe to Justice Corn the previous year. Cargill, without telling Carroll about his role in obtaining Carlile's vote, simply told his client that Cargill could have handled the bribe for less money.

Somehow Carroll would also have to explain in court the two-hundred-thousand-dollar alleged loan. Cargill refused to allow Carroll to consider taking the Fifth Amendment on the subject and insisted Carroll testify to a different, more creative version of the facts. Apparently after discussing a vacation home the Carrolls owned in Canada, Cargill and Carroll concocted a lie about Carroll's lending the money to Pierre Laval, a fictional French-Canadian oilman who had then disappeared with the money. Julia Carroll, who had taken a serious dislike to Cargill, strongly objected to this preposterous story about a nonexistent person, but the overbearing and forceful Cargill insisted.[58]

At the March 17 hearing Carroll indeed testified that he gave the money to one Pierre Laval, an oil speculator whom he had met at Lake of the Woods in Canada.[59] Because the transaction took place in Canada, according to Carroll's testimony, a check was not acceptable, so he had cashed a check in Oklahoma and then flown to Canada to meet with Laval. Laval did not sign a promissory note, and no paperwork was exchanged. Carroll testified he did not get an address or phone number for Laval; he had given the Canadian the money, and Laval had simply disappeared, leaving Carroll to feel he had "bought the Brooklyn Bridge." At the same hearing, Selected's sales director admitted he had withdrawn his own money from Selected Investments the previous July, even though he and the company were still advertising Selected's services to the general public.[60]

The next week the public heard more about the financial affairs of Selected Investments. Paul Duncan, the bankruptcy trustee, subpoenaed Robert O. Cunningham, a former Oklahoma City legislator who had opposed the company in the 1951 dispute with Cope. Things had changed, however, in the subsequent years; Cunningham had borrowed over six hundred thousand dollars from the company to finance a telephone directory business. The business had failed, and Selected had written off about four hundred thousand dollars of Cunningham's debt without making a serious effort to collect it. The trustee also established that Carroll and his son-in-law William Rigg, who was a vice president of Selected, had pocketed payments from the city of Oklahoma City intended for Selected on a residential development.

By March 27 the bankruptcy hearings had confirmed what everyone had suspected. The corporate officers of Selected Investments had taken investor money and not invested it at all. Instead, they had paid the promised returns with money from new investors while squandering hundreds of thousands of dollars on exorbitant compensation for employees, personal expenses, and ill-advised and shady business ventures. By the next year Carroll and Burns were in a federal penitentiary. Even while incarcerated, Carroll stuck to the Pierre Laval fiction and kept the secret of the bribery. Fortunately, through the efforts of the bankruptcy attorneys, the investors in Selected Investments recovered about two-thirds of their money.[61]

❖ 3
Prosecution and the Seeds of Reform

After the late 1950s the sordid story of Selected Investments gradually fell out of the public eye. Hugh Carroll and Phil Burns went to federal prison and served their sentences; the investors received most of their money back. So far as the general public knew, the case was over. Although the *Selected Investments* case itself no longer occupied the public's attention, Oklahomans in general had become disillusioned and dissatisfied with the insider-friendly nature of their state government. The state's population also became more urban, and residents of the more populous areas resented the control that rural politicians held at the state capitol.

In 1958 thirty-three year-old J. Howard Edmondson, astutely and effectively employing the new medium of television, was elected to the governor's office on a reform platform. Edmondson advocated modernization in nearly every aspect of state government, including reform in highway administration, a merit system for selection of state employees, central purchasing of state equipment and supplies, the end of Prohibition, and removal of secondary offices from the ballot.[1] The new governor's platform and the election of a young outsider like Edmondson constituted breaks with the rural southern populism that had dominated the state for its first half-century. In addition to his platform, Edmondson's urbane style contrasted greatly with his immediate two predecessors, Raymond Gary and Johnston Murray.

Surprisingly, Edmondson's gubernatorial papers show little or no discussion of judicial reform. Edmondson was an attorney and a politician, and he would have been aware of the rumors regarding the Supreme Court. However, the scandal would not be exposed until after Edmondson left office, and the governor already had a lot on his plate. Edmondson was only able to achieve the repeal of Prohibition by, among other tactics, well-publicized raids of country clubs, which were illegally selling alcohol to members and their guests. This and his battle for passage of a merit system for hiring state employees took an enormous political toll. It therefore seems likely that Edmondson allowed court reform, which had not yet captured the public's imagination, to take a backseat to his other proposals.²

Although Edmondson had entered office with high hopes and riding a wave of public approval, neither he nor the electorate had anticipated the Oklahoma legislature's power to resist his plans. Although he was able to enact the repeal of Prohibition, central purchasing, and the merit system, Edmondson quickly lost control of the Democratic Party to the rural, conservative majority in the legislature. Edmondson could blame himself for part of the problem; he and his aides had unnecessarily alienated legislators and others with their brash style, youthful arrogance, and disregard for tradition and protocol. By the end of his term, the conservative legislature had completely overwhelmed Governor Edmondson, who survived the repeal of the newly passed merit system only with the assistance of House Speaker J. D. McCarty.³ However voters felt about Edmondson's administration, they remained restive and receptive to the possibility of major change.

In 1962, traditionally Democratic Oklahoma voters again expressed their dissatisfaction with their state government by electing Billings farmer Henry Bellmon as the state's first Republican governor, providing another chink in the armor of the dominance of rural Democrats. As the state chair of the Oklahoma Republican Party, Bellmon had energized his troops by naming new leadership to the party and appealing to younger, urban voters. Bellmon exploited hostility and dissension among the Democrats, swamping W. P. (Bill) Atkinson, the millionaire developer of Midwest City, who had narrowly defeated former governor Raymond Gary in a bitter runoff for the Democratic nomination.⁴ In his term Bellmon would also encounter frustration with the Democratic legislature and clash bitterly with Speaker McCarty.

Prosecution of N. S. Corn

Although the public controversy had died down, the federal government had not forgotten about Selected Investments, the missing two hundred thousand dollars at the hands of the mysterious and elusive Pierre Laval, and the Supreme Court's bewildering and suspicious decision in favor of Selected. Spurred by a tip that two justices were evading federal income taxes, B. Andrew Potter—the U.S. attorney for the Western District of Oklahoma—and the IRS continued to investigate.⁵ Although he originally had insufficient evidence to justify a prosecution, Potter continued to pursue Hugh Carroll, who had been released from federal prison. The state of Oklahoma still had the right to prosecute Carroll for his Selected Investments crimes, so Carroll also feared state prosecution. In March 1964, enticed by the possibility of a pardon and a promise of immunity from state prosecution, Carroll finally spoke with the IRS. He and his wife, Julia, also gave statements to County Attorney Jim Harrod and Assistant County Attorney John Amick.[6] The next month Potter began to press his case to a federal grand jury.[7]

N. S. Corn and Earl Welch were also feeling pressure from the IRS and Potter. Corn had quietly dealt with the IRS since at least 1962, and had privately indicated to the authorities that, if indicted, he would not contest criminal charges. Between the summers of 1962 and 1964, Corn, still serving as a supernumerary judge for the Oklahoma Supreme Court, paid the government nearly twenty thousand dollars in overdue taxes, penalties, and interest while preparing for bad news from the federal authorities.[8]

In the meantime, the longtime relationship between Corn and O. A. Cargill finally ruptured. At Cargill's suggestion, Corn retained Oklahoma City tax attorney John Speck to represent him in his troubles with the IRS. According to Corn, Speck and Cargill contacted Corn and indicated that his troubles with the IRS would go away for twenty thousand dollars, implying they had bribed an IRS agent. Corn concluded that Speck and Cargill were trying to scam him. Corn later claimed he had angrily refused the offer and ended his attorney-client relationship with Speck. Whatever the facts, Corn and Cargill's corrupt friendship ended in bitterness and acrimony.[9]

U.S. district judge Roy Harper presided over the grand jury. Harper, a former small-town lawyer, was a veteran of Democratic Party politics in Missouri, where he had been chair of the state party. In 1947 President Harry Truman, a fellow Missourian, appointed him to the federal bench. After the local judges recused themselves, Harper was sent to Oklahoma in January 1964 to hear what he thought would be one case: W. H. (Pat) O'Bryan's libel suit against Judge Chandler, which had arisen from O'Bryan's claim for a million-dollar fee in the Selected Investments bankruptcy. As it happened, Harper was assigned to most of the litigation that developed from the scandal and spent many months in Oklahoma.[10]

On April 6, 1964, the federal grand jury began hearing from witnesses who knew about the financial affairs of Corn and Welch, including Hugh Carroll and Welch's ex-wife, Fern. The next day Welch himself appeared and testified for about two hours, then continued his testimony for most of the next day. After Welch's testimony concluded, the grand jury indicted Corn and Welch on five charges each of income tax evasion. The next day Welch released a statement strongly denying his guilt and any inappropriate involvement with Selected Investments.[11] Two weeks later, Corn and Welch appeared in Oklahoma City federal court; Welch pleaded not guilty and successfully demanded his trial be moved to the Eastern District of Oklahoma, where he officially lived. When Justice Corn's turn came before the bench, he and his attorney attempted to plead "no defense," citing concerns for the eighty-year-old defendant's health.[12] Judge Harper refused to hear Corn's no-defense plea, and Corn's attorney then entered a plea of not guilty for his client.[13]

On July 1, Corn reappeared before Judge Harper, this time pleading nolo contendere to evading taxes for the years 1956, 1958, and 1959 and to filing false returns for two of those years. Corn's lawyer, James Eagleton, insisted to the judge that Corn was guilty only of technical violations of the law. Eagleton stuck to Corn's statements to the IRS agents: that he had earned his undeclared income from winnings on poker with players he declined to identify and from gambling on horse races. According to Eagleton, the only reason for his client's no contest plea was his ill health and physical inability to stand trial.[14]

Eagleton's misleading statement was too much for U.S. attorney B. Andrew Potter. After clearing the action with U.S. attorney general Robert F. Kennedy, Potter responded by telling the court that Corn had taken a $150,000 bribe. This bombshell announcement was the first notice to the general public of allegations of corruption in the Oklahoma Supreme Court. After Potter's statement, Harper immediately sentenced Corn to a term of eighteen months but set another hearing to determine whether Corn was physically able to withstand incarceration.[15]

N. S. Corn was now a convicted felon sentenced to prison. He was also a supernumerary judge for the Oklahoma Supreme Court, drawing a salary of $9,374 per year from Oklahoma taxpayers. This fact illustrated a glaring weakness in Oklahoma's political structure that would be further exposed in the cases of Welch and Johnson: the inability to discipline or terminate corrupt or incompetent officials. Corn, no longer an elected justice, was a salaried supernumerary judge appointed by the governor with case assignments determined by the Supreme Court. Despite this, neither the governor nor the justices had the power to terminate him. Only the legislature, which would not convene until the next year, could remove Corn by the expensive and time-consuming avenue of impeachment.

Chief Justice W. H. Blackbird telephoned Corn on the day of his plea and demanded his resignation. Corn stalled Blackbird, stating he would think about the subject for a few days. Blackbird admitted to an interviewer that he did not know what the court would do if Corn refused to resign. In the meantime, Potter's vague courtroom disclosure, with the implication that other still unnamed justices may have been involved in a bribery scheme, cast an intolerable shadow on the reputation of the Supreme Court and those justices who were innocent of any wrongdoing.[16]

Even before Corn's plea, reform groups had been calling for greater judicial accountability. In November 1963 a group led by lawyers and University of Oklahoma law professor Maurice Merrill formed the Oklahoma Institute for Justice Inc., a nonprofit corporation dedicated to establishing a court to oversee the judiciary and reform in judicial selection.[17] By April the group had hired an Oklahoma Baptist University professor as its full-time director and had prepared State Question 415, a constitutional amendment directing the establishment of a court on the judiciary.[18] The movement gained momentum after Corn's highly publicized plea and sentencing.[19]

On July 4, Corn finally resigned his position as supernumerary judge. His failure to resign from the Oklahoma Bar Association led to a hastily called and chaotic meeting of the leadership of the bar association and the Supreme Court. Wielding a cigar, Justice Welch, who had himself been indicted the previous week, attended the meeting, cryptically saying it was "best to lay these things on the table." Justice Johnson, whose involvement in the scandal was not yet public knowledge, also attended.[20]

After the meeting ended with a general agreement that the Oklahoma Bar Association (OBA) should begin disbarment proceedings against Corn, Justice Welch called Floyd Rheam, a Tulsa attorney who had chaired the meeting, and told Rheam that Corn would resign from the bar. Rheam went directly to Corn's home, which was a few blocks south of the capitol. When Rheam entered the residence, he noticed Earl Welch standing in a back room. Corn handed Rheam a handwritten resignation letter. In a voice that Welch could easily hear, Corn told Rheam "to tell the Executive Council [of the OBA] that I never gave money to a judge or any member of the Supreme Court for any purpose."[21]

Investigations of judicial misconduct now came from everywhere. In addition to Welch's criminal case scheduled for trial in October, Governor Bellmon, calling Corn's plea "sickening and despicable corruption in the highest judicial court of our state," directed Dale Cook, his legal aide and a future federal judge, to undertake his own inquiry. Oklahoma County Attorney

James Harrod announced the possibility of a grand jury probe into the matter. The OBA appointed a committee of three attorneys to investigate the case as well.[22] The Supreme Court granted subpoena power to the OBA investigators, over Harrod's objection, who pointed out the inconsistency of the Supreme Court granting subpoena power to investigate itself.[23] In September Governor Bellmon appointed yet another panel, this one composed of nonlawyers and charged with serving as a watchdog over the bar committee.[24]

On July 29, having received an inconclusive medical report on Corn's physical ability to withstand incarceration, Judge Harper ordered the defendant transported to prison. A veteran of the rough-and-tumble world of Missouri politics, Harper seemed not to be particularly shocked by Corn's crimes and demonstrated considerable sensitivity to Corn's medical condition. Even though he admitted he had no judicial authority to select where Corn would be incarcerated, he did it anyway. Judge Harper arranged for Corn to be housed at the federal facility for infirm inmates in Springfield, Missouri. He also ordered the federal marshal to bypass transporting Corn to the county jail and to pick up his prisoner at Corn's home. Harper told the parties that if any change occurred in Corn's condition within the next sixty days, the parties should let him know and he would "return this man to his home.... Because as I said, this isn't the death penalty." He authorized the federal parole board to parole Corn at any time it deemed appropriate. Corn cryptically told a reporter that the result of the hearing was "the best thing."[25] The marshal took Corn to Springfield, and he began his term on that day.

Corn was eighty years old. He was also frail, having survived a serious heart attack and colon cancer. Nevertheless, the undisputed facts were that an Oklahoma Supreme Court justice had drastically understated his income to the IRS, then refused to disclose the source of the money. Corn neither confirmed nor denied the government's alarming assertion that he had received a large bribe; instead, he remained silent in the face of such a serious allegation. Under these circumstances, Judge Harper's solicitous attitude toward Corn, the chief suspect in a huge bribery case, seems unusually accommodating. Had Harper pressured Corn harder, the truth might have come out more quickly.

The Trial of Earl Welch

Judge Harper's next Oklahoma assignment was the trial of Justice Welch, which began on October 5, 1964, in Muskogee.[26] Born in 1892 Earl Welch grew up in small towns in the Choctaw Nation, in what is now southeastern

Oklahoma. Welch's father and grandfather were lawyers, and Welch spent much of his childhood around their small-town law offices. Although he had attended law school at the University of Oklahoma, finances forced him to leave prior to graduation. Instead, he read for the bar privately at his father's and grandfather's offices, then successfully sat for the bar examination. In 1911, four years after Oklahoma achieved statehood, Welch became a lawyer and established an office in his hometown of Antlers.[27]

During his years in private practice, Welch became involved in the murky and morally questionable business of trading in Indian land.[28] Much of this business was conducted in cash, a practice that, along with Welch's excessive spending financed through mysterious infusions of currency, would become an issue at Welch's trial fifty years later.[29] Despite his claims many years after the fact, Welch and his wife, Fern, lived frugally during their twenty years in Antlers. While Welch was in private practice, he did his own stenographic and janitorial work. The family lived in a modest, sparsely furnished home, where they raised their own vegetables. For several years, especially in the 1920s, they did not own a car. They never entertained. It seems clear that during Welch's private-practice years in Antlers, he was only moderately financially successful.[30]

In 1926 Welch was elected district judge for his district in southeastern Oklahoma. Six years later he announced his candidacy for the Democratic nomination for the Oklahoma Supreme Court, opposing incumbent Earl Lester for the southeastern Oklahoma seat. The 1932 election proved to be an exception to the rule that judicial races were issueless: the issue in this election was Governor William H. Murray, whose megalomania, eccentric behavior, intolerance of dissent, and misuse of martial law had exhausted his goodwill with the Oklahoma voters. Murray endorsed Lester; in a rebuke of Governor Murray, incumbents statewide were defeated for reelection.[31] Lester was one of the incumbents to fall, and Welch became a member of the Oklahoma Supreme Court in January 1933. As a member of the Chickasaw Nation, Welch became the first enrolled Native American to sit on any state's highest court.[32]

There is no evidence of extraordinary spending by Welch in his early years on the court.[33] In the late 1940s, however, Welch began an intimate relationship with Ruby Myers, and Justice Welch became the primary, if not sole, source of her financial support. Ruby rented an apartment next to her sister and brother-in-law, Ophia and W. S. Taylor, on North Robinson

Avenue in Oklahoma City. Welch was a frequent visitor to Ruby's apartment. Although Ruby had no employment or other source of income, her rent was always promptly paid.[34]

In 1953 Ruby and the Taylors bought a home in that same neighborhood; Welch had looked at the home with the potential buyers and later attended the closing on the property.[35] Taylor paid $6,000 down for the home, although the retired airline employee's income was only $76.80 from Social Security. Ruby Myers also paid about $1,800 as a down payment, the money coming from an unexplained source. During the late 1950s the Taylors moved to Arizona for two years. Despite their absence, Ruby, although she was unemployed, was able to make the payments on the home.[36]

In December 1958 Fern and Earl Welch divorced. On June 27, 1959, one week after the expiration of Oklahoma's six-month waiting period, Welch and Ruby Myers married in Las Vegas.[37] Investigators later learned that during the late 1950s, Ruby spent approximately thirty-eight hundred dollars at Balliet's, a fashionable Oklahoma City women's clothing store. Most of the bills were paid personally by Ruby's sister, Ophia Taylor, in one-hundred-dollar bills, with no explanation provided for the source of the money.[38] Suspiciously, for many years Welch kept a safety deposit box at the First National Bank of Oklahoma City. Between 1956 and 1960 Welch entered the safety deposit box ten or twelve times per year, activities that Welch could not explain several years later.[39]

In 1962 the Internal Revenue Service began looking into Welch's financial affairs. An investigator scheduled an interview with Welch for May 17. Bank records later revealed that Welch entered his safety deposit box on that very day. The agent made another appointment with Justice Welch on August 29; Welch opened the box on the following day, August 30.[40] Welch had no explanation for these suspicious events either.

Welch's criminal trial, which began on October 5, 1964, was a strange event that became more notable for the evidence the jury did not hear, rather than what the jury heard. Everyone knew the true issue: the government believed Welch had been supplementing his income by accepting bribes, including in the *Selected Investments* case. He had been using the bribe money, according to the government, to maintain both his households in a relatively comfortable, although not elaborate, way. However, the jurors never heard any testimony regarding this theory.

The prosecution's case had serious flaws. Hugh Carroll, fearful of further prosecution, had made a complete statement to the authorities regarding his role in the Selected bribery. However, Carroll had never dealt with Welch; his only knowledge of Corn's purchase of Welch's vote came from Corn and was therefore hearsay. Carroll could testify he had bribed Corn. He could not testify he had bribed Welch, only that he had ultimately received Welch's vote. As for Corn, he had been sentenced to prison after his no-contest plea to tax evasion; he had admitted only to the tax improprieties, not bribery. Corn had not been charged with accepting the bribes, nor had he yet made any admission to law enforcement authorities on that subject.

The case against Welch that the jurors heard was as follows: Welch had overspent his income without a valid explanation, had given misleading statements to investigators, had suspiciously entered his safety deposit box, and had made an inordinate number of expenditures in cash, especially one-hundred-dollar bills. The government's case was methodical and tedious, going all the way back to Welch's opening his law office in 1911, using business records to demonstrate the extent to which Welch had overspent his income.[41] V. P. Crowe, Welch's tough and capable lawyer, implied that Welch had earned large sums of cash dealing in the unethical and immoral business of early Oklahoma Indian land titles. According to Crowe's theory, Welch had simply taken the cash with him when he moved to Oklahoma City in 1932, leaving it in his safety deposit box and taking some of the money from time to time.

Outside of the jury's hearing, completely different issues arose. On the fifth day of the trial, the government called Corn, who had been returned to Muskogee from the federal prison in Springfield, Missouri, to testify. Judge Harper sent the jury out of the courtroom and heard Corn's testimony. The feeble and disheveled Corn, who had not been prosecuted or charged directly for any bribery case, invoked the Fifth Amendment seventeen times.[42] The next day Hugh Carroll, the former president of Selected Investments, testified, also outside the presence of the jury. For the first time, the sordid story of the Selected Investments bribery came out publicly in the words of a participant. However, since Carroll had not dealt directly with Welch in any way, Judge Harper ruled his testimony inadmissible against Welch.[43]

On October 19, after deliberating less than two hours, the jury convicted Welch on all counts.[44] When he appeared for his sentencing three weeks later, Welch strongly denied taking any bribe at any time in his career and pleaded for leniency on behalf of his wife and his disabled son. Judge Harper sentenced Welch to three years' imprisonment on each case, with the sentences to run concurrently, and to pay fines totaling $13,500. Harper authorized prison authorities to parole Welch at any time they deemed appropriate and allowed Welch to remain free on bond pending his appeal of his conviction.[45]

The judge took the opportunity to blast Welch's supporters, who had been contacting the jurors in an attempt to obtain information with which to impeach the jury's verdict. Curiously, Harper stated from the bench that he had "never seen a simpler tax case" or "seen one with less actual defense."[46] Unfortunately, Harper did not require Welch to resign his judicial post in order to remain free on bond, an omission that caused considerable expense and significant misery for Oklahoma's legislature and governor.

The Failure of State Question 415

On October 21, the day after Welch's conviction, Governor Bellmon announced that he was considering calling a special session of the legislature to impeach Justice Welch, who—despite having been found guilty of felonies—remained a duly elected member of the Oklahoma Supreme Court.[47] Bellmon qualified his remarks by endorsing State Question 415 (SQ 415), the proposed constitutional amendment establishing a court on the judiciary, which would be on voters' general election ballot on November 3. The governor indicated the special session would not be necessary if the voters passed the constitutional amendment.[48]

Supporters of the state question establishing the court on the judiciary had reason to be cautiously optimistic. Bellmon spoke strongly in favor of it.[49] Almost every newspaper in the state heartily endorsed the measure, with the powerful *Daily Oklahoman* and *Tulsa Tribune* being particularly forceful. The *Tribune*, the newspaper that may have been the most enthusiastic about the proposal, titled one editorial "If Not Now, When?"[50] Smaller papers, like the *Norman Transcript* and the *Daily Ardmoreite*, also urged their readers to vote in favor of SQ 415.[51] The Cleveland County Bar Association sent speakers to civic clubs urging the amendment's passage, with one local trial judge pointing out to his audience the logic of reform that "is free," the only expense to the taxpayers being mileage and meal expense.[52] The Garfield County Bar Association purchased a full-page advertisement in the Enid newspaper endorsing the proposal.[53] It was difficult to find a good reason to support the idea of retaining convicted judges in office, so SQ 415 encountered no significant opposition from the general public or the statewide press.

However, SQ 415's backers also recognized two significant problems with its passage. The first roadblock, which proved to be fatal to the amendment, was the silent vote. All political pundits predicted a heavy turnout for the 1964 election, which featured the presidential election between Lyndon Johnson and Barry Goldwater and a hotly contested U.S. Senate contest between Democrat Fred R. Harris and Republican Bud Wilkinson.[54] Oklahoma's constitution provided that any amendment must pass by a majority of all votes cast, not simply those voting on that particular measure. If a voter voted for president or U.S. Senate and failed to vote on SQ 415, that vote therefore counted as a "no" vote. In a year like 1964, the silent vote could kill the state question.

SQ 415 also happened to have been placed on the ballot with six other state questions. The questions appeared in numerical order, with 415 appearing just after a wildly unpopular proposal to increase legislative salaries. Two controversial education measures also appeared, strongly endorsed by the Oklahoma Education Association and Speaker McCarty and vociferously opposed by Governor Bellmon. In order to secure approval of SQ 415, its backers would have the burden of educating voters about the pressing need to remove corrupt judges and to navigate through the minefields of the federal elections and the distraction caused by the other state questions.

Oklahoma's 1964 general election turnout was indeed very high. Oklahoma voters voted 56 percent for Johnson; Goldwater only narrowly carried traditionally Republican Tulsa County while losing conservative Oklahoma County. Johnson's margin of victory in the state, which exceeded 110,000 votes, helped carry the young and energetic Fred R. Harris, who had campaigned on his close relationship to the White House, over Bud Wilkinson, the articulate and popular former Oklahoma Sooner football coach.[55]

State Question 415 failed. Although 397,823 voters approved the measure and 370,604 voted against it, the high turnout and the silent vote defeated SQ 415.[56] Since 949,330 Oklahomans went to the polls, 474,666 votes had been necessary to obtain a majority of all votes. State Question 415, although it did better than all the other state questions on the ballot and won majorities in nineteen counties, including the most populous ones, therefore came nowhere close to passage.

The failure of SQ 415 also illustrates the instinctive and inherent opposition of Oklahomans of that time period to political change. Even in the midst of an enormous judicial scandal and without organized opposition, 48 percent of those who actually voted on the proposal cast their ballots against it. A combination of Oklahoma's antireform constitutional structure and general public skepticism killed State Question 415, and the court on the judiciary was not approved.

After the election, the silent vote came under considerable criticism. The *Tulsa Tribune*, which had pushed so hard for SQ 415's enactment, blamed the proposal's defeat on the confusing nature of the ballot and on the silent vote, reasonably arguing, "Who could possibly have opposed State Question 415?" State Senator Dewey Bartlett, who became Oklahoma's next governor, also advocated for elimination of the silent vote.[57] Ten years later, in 1974, Oklahoma voters finally abolished it.[58]

Governor Bellmon, frustrated by the fact that Justice Welch remained in office and on the public payroll, again strongly considered the idea of convening a special session of the legislature for the purpose of impeaching and removing him. McCarty and incoming Senate president pro tempore Clem McSpadden opposed the idea, pointing out that by the time the special session could be called, the regular session would be only six weeks away. In this case McCarty and McSpadden proved to be the cooler heads, and Bellmon did not call the legislature into special session. Welch's future as a member of the court would become the problem of the reapportioned 1965 legislature.[59]

On December 10 the Oklahoma Supreme Court took the symbolic, if superfluous, step of suspending Welch's law license, finding that Welch's felony conviction barred him from practicing law. As Welch himself pointed out, he had been legally barred from practicing law since 1927 by the fact of his holding judicial office. Under Oklahoma law, therefore, even though Welch was no longer even a licensed attorney, he remained a member of the Oklahoma Supreme Court, the same body that had suspended his license. He received his salary and remained a full, if inactive, justice.[60]

Meanwhile, N. S. Corn was using his testimony as a bargaining chip for his release from prison. On December 2, at the suggestion of IRS attorney Willard McBride, outgoing county attorney James Harrod and an assistant drove to the federal prison in Springfield to speak to Corn about the possibility of Corn's making a statement to the authorities. Corn told Harrod he would cooperate on the conditions that his statement remain confidential with no copies made, and that his family would be protected. Harrod agreed to those conditions, although he almost certainly had no authority to agree to the confidentiality provision and would prove to have trouble living up to that commitment.[61]

On December 9, U.S. Attorney B. Andrew Potter, Harrod, several government attorneys, Corn's attorney Dick Fowler, and a court reporter traveled to Springfield. Corn gave the lawyers an exhaustive, eighty-two-page statement, in which he described the details of the bribery scandal. Nine days later, having served only four months in prison, Corn was released on parole. In exchange for Corn's statement and anticipated testimony, Harrod, who was leaving office in three weeks, assured Corn of immunity from state prosecution.[62]

While the fact soon became public that Corn had given a statement to law enforcement, the authorities originally honored their confidentiality agreement, and the specific contents of his confession remained undisclosed and unavailable.[63] On January 5, 1965, Corn testified before a closed Oklahoma Bar Association committee investigating the scandal. This testimony also remained private.[64] Harrod later considered his confidentiality promise to be moot when a law school classmate employed by O. A. Cargill showed him a letter Corn had written Cargill, which said in part, "Dear O.A., Don't mess with my family. I've told them everything." Corn, who had demanded the confidentiality, had violated the agreement himself.[65] As it happened, Corn's statement remained confidential for only a few weeks. To the horror of Oklahomans, the size of the scandal would become even more apparent during the coming year.

Representative G. T. Blankenship in 1960. Blankenship later served as the attorney general of Oklahoma. Courtesy of the Oklahoma Historical Society.

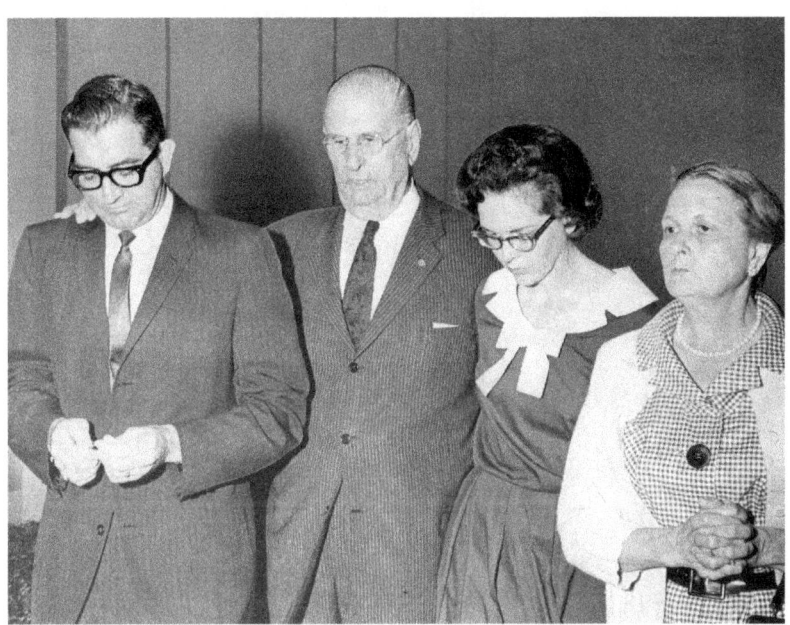

O. A. Cargill leaving the courthouse with his family after his conviction in federal court. Courtesy of the Oklahoma Historical Society.

Selected Investments president Hugh Carroll and his wife, Julia, in court in 1958. Courtesy of the Oklahoma Historical Society.

Justice N. S. Corn. Courtesy of the Oklahoma Historical Society.

Senator Roy Grantham presiding at Justice N. B. Johnson's 1965 impeachment trial. Courtesy of the Oklahoma Historical Society.

Johnson listening at his impeachment trial. Courtesy of the Oklahoma Historical Society.

Speaker of the House J. D. McCarty. Courtesy of the Oklahoma Historical Society.

Justice Earl Welch in the state capitol. Courtesy of the Oklahoma Historical Society.

Representative Burke G. Mordy, chief counsel for the house investigating committee. From William A. Berry and James Edwin Alexander, *Justice for Sale: The Shocking Scandal of the Oklahoma Supreme Court* (Oklahoma City: Macedon, 1996), n.p.

The 1953 Oklahoma Supreme Court. Author's collection.

❖ 4

The 1965 Legislature and the Impeachment of N. B. Johnson

On January 5, 1965, the Thirtieth Session of the Oklahoma legislature convened. Governor Bellmon delivered his State of the State address, proposing a program he called Operation Giant Stride, which included an extensive list of proposed reforms, including highways, education, mental health, welfare, congressional redistricting, and public safety. For some reason Bellmon, who only two months earlier had wanted to call a special session in order to impeach Earl Welch, did not mention Welch's remarkable status as a convicted felon on the state's highest court, nor did he give any attention to the state's court system.[1] Bellmon may have been trying to avoid early conflict with Speaker McCarty, who had predicted tough sledding for the movement to impeach Welch. McCarty argued that Welch's case remained on appeal and cited a general lack of legislative enthusiasm for the project.[2]

Because of recent rulings from the U.S. Supreme Court, the makeup of the Oklahoma legislature differed drastically from previous legislatures. As the country became more and more urbanized in the mid-twentieth century, state legislatures, which were dominated by rural areas, became less representative of the population. Although many states, including Oklahoma, had constitutional or statutory requirements that the legislature periodically reapportion itself, state legislatures tended to ignore those mandates, which would diminish the power of rural legislators and, in many cases, reallocate their seats to urban areas. By the 1940s legislative reapportionment had become a major issue in American politics and law.

In 1946 the U.S. Supreme Court considered reapportionment in *Colegrove v. Green,* which involved a challenge to the apportionment of the Illinois legislature. The Court decided that apportionment of legislatures was a political issue to be determined by the states and not by the courts. Justice Felix Frankfurter, the conservative author of the opinion, declared, "Courts ought not to enter this political thicket."[3] Sixteen years later the Supreme Court ignored Frankfurter's advice and entered the thicket with a vengeance.

By 1962 the political times had changed, as had the makeup of the court. The 1960 election of John F. Kennedy also meant that a more liberal Department of Justice took an active and aggressive role in challenging failure to reapportion. Future Watergate prosecutor Archibald Cox took the lead for the government. The case at issue was *Baker v. Carr*, in which well-financed and aggressive attorneys for the plaintiff challenged the makeup of Tennessee's legislature. Following the precedent of *Colegrove*, the district court and the circuit court of appeals ruled that the courts had no jurisdiction over legislative apportionment. Under the U.S. Supreme Court rules, four justices were required to accept the case for argument in order for it to be heard at that level. When liberal justices Earl Warren, Hugo Black, William O. Douglas, and William Brennan voted to accept the case, the subject of reapportionment was again before the court.

Baker v. Carr proved to be extremely controversial and saw bitter infighting within the Supreme Court itself, with Justice Frankfurter forcefully lobbying his colleagues to rule that the courts did not have jurisdiction. The Court was so divided that at the request of Justice Potter Stewart, who was undecided, the court heard oral arguments twice. The pressure grew so great that Justice Charles Evans Whittaker, who had been suffering from depression, entered the hospital and retired from the court before the vote. Justice Tom Clark told Frankfurter he would prepare an opinion denying jurisdiction, then changed his mind about the issue and voted for the plaintiffs.[4] Eventually, in an opinion Brennan wrote, the court ruled that legislative apportionment involved the Fourteenth Amendment guarantee of equal protection of the law and was therefore subject to the jurisdiction of the courts.[5]

As Frankfurter had predicted, *Baker v. Carr* opened the floodgates to Supreme Court litigation, and the court received petitions from cases involving several states, including Colorado, Delaware, Alabama, Maryland, New York, and Virginia.[6] In 1964 the court considered a resolution to these cases by deciding the Alabama case, *Reynolds v. Sims*. On June 15, 1964, Chief Justice Warren read the court's opinion. Warren compared malapportionment to the practice of allowing some residents to vote five or ten times, then famously stated, "Legislators represent people, not trees or acres. Legislators are elected by voters, not farms or cities or economic interests." According to the Supreme Court, the Fourteenth Amendment required that state legislatures be apportioned by population. The opinion also barred the practice of some states, including Oklahoma, of guaranteeing at least one representative per county.[7]

The Court's decision forcing reapportionment of state legislatures met with considerable resistance from those who objected to the expansion of federal power, especially judicial power, at the expense of the states. Presidential candidate Barry Goldwater vociferously objected to the ruling. The Republican Party registered its objection to Reynolds v. Sims in the party's 1964 platform, endorsing the idea of a constitutional amendment allowing states to apportion one house of bicameral legislatures "on bases of their choosing, including factors other than population."[8] A proposal to support the court's decisions in the Democratic Party platform was killed by Representative Carl Albert, the majority leader of the U.S. House, who represented a rural Oklahoma district.[9]

The leader of the opposition to the apportionment decisions was Illinois senator Everett Dirksen, the minority leader of the U.S. Senate. At considerable political cost, Dirksen had just helped end a filibuster to the 1964 Civil Rights Act and negotiated the successful passage of the civil rights bill acceptable to most Senate Republicans. To Dirksen, a native of the small town of Pekin, Illinois, the reapportionment cases constituted a threat to the political power and autonomy of rural America. The issue also provided Dirksen an opportunity to mend fences with the fast-rising Goldwater wing of the Republican Party.

Dirksen introduced a proposed amendment to the U.S. Constitution, allowing each state to apportion one house of their legislatures in a manner they deemed appropriate. He also proposed a bill to delay the implementation of the reapportionment decision, a constitutionally dubious move that was eventually killed by the vote of Paul Douglas, Dirksen's fellow Illinois senator.[10] Dirksen then proposed legislation that would allow state voters to decide the composition of their own legislature, a bill that also nearly passed the Senate.[11] Eventually he refocused his efforts on states calling for a constitutional convention to remedy the problem, an effort that came within one state of adoption. When Dirksen died in 1969 the resistance to reapportionment gradually disappeared.[12]

Oklahoma's experience with legislative reapportionment had been contentious and bitter. Although the state's constitution required the legislature to be reapportioned every ten years, the House of Representatives had not reapportioned itself since 1921, and the Senate had never done so.[13] Political scientists ranked Oklahoma forty-seventh of the fifty states in terms of malapportionment.[14] In 1956 the legislature considered the issue, but the passage of reapportionment was blocked by the rurally oriented governor Raymond Gary. Gary's successor, J. Howard Edmondson, favored reapportioning one legislative house by area and the other by population, but the proposal did not become law.

In the early 1960s two separate reapportionment measures were submitted to Oklahoma voters; both proposals failed. Until ordered to do so by the courts, the state election board, led by an Edmondson appointee and a Republican, refused to accept legislative filings for the 1962 election, claiming that the apportionment of the districts was unconstitutional. In the general election that year, Edmondson submitted a proposal to the voters creating an administrative commission to handle reapportionment. Although a majority of voters cast their ballots in favor of the proposal in the general election, the silent vote killed the measure.

Pressure from the federal courts, including the U.S. Supreme Court, finally led to reapportionment in Oklahoma. The federal district court in Oklahoma City ordered the Oklahoma legislature to reapportion itself equitably by March 8, 1963, a deadline the legislature met with a halfhearted effort that still allowed for disproportionate representation and was quickly overturned by the federal courts. The Oklahoma Supreme Court then issued a plan that deviated only slightly from the original legislative plan. In May 1964 the state voted for legislators running for office under the Supreme Court's plan.

The next month, the U.S. Supreme Court upheld the power of the federal courts to supervise reapportionment in Oklahoma. The federal court vacated the May election results and ordered a new election for September under districts apportioned under a plan it approved.[15] The urban districts in the plan were drawn by Patience Latting, a future Oklahoma City mayor who had an advanced degree in statistics and had been active in the reapportionment movement through her involvement with the League of Women Voters.[16] This plan prevailed, and the 1965 legislature comprised those districts.

As a result of reapportionment, the 1965 legislature differed drastically from its predecessors. More than half of the 1963 legislature did not return for the next session.[17] The guarantee of one representative per county was gone, replaced by numbered districts that often included more than one county. The previous legislature had comprised 119 members of the House of Representatives and 36 senators; the 1965 version contained 99 members of the House of Representatives and 46 senators. In 1963 Oklahoma County and Tulsa County had been represented by only one senator each, with Oklahoma County having seven members of the House. The 1965 version had nine senators from Oklahoma County and seven from Tulsa County. Eighteen members of the House of Representatives represented Oklahoma County, with fifteen from Tulsa County. For the first time since 1910, the legislature contained African Americans.

From the standpoint of representation by political party, the legislature had barely changed. The 1963 session had been composed of 86.4 percent Democrats in the Senate and 79.8 percent in the House. The Thirtieth legislature convened in January 1965 with 85.4 percent Democrats in the Senate and 77.8 percent in the House. The legislative leadership primarily remained in rural hands. Nevertheless, the conclusion is inescapable: the legislature had become more urban and less beholden to rural interests. The entry of new membership into both houses, who owed their seats to outside pressure for change, enlarged the constituency for reform.[18]

Pressure from outside the Leadership

Although the Democratic legislative leadership clearly wanted nothing to do with the issue of Justice Welch's removal from the court, events were moving beyond leadership's control. On January 4, 1965, the Oklahoma Supreme Court had begun its new term. Although he had not been participating in court business since his indictment, Welch appeared in the court's conference room and cryptically announced, "I don't think I had better attend the conferences, but I will tell you how you can dispose of cases where you won't need my vote." Welch's unsolicited appearance and breezy attitude infuriated Justice William A. Berry, who had defeated Lon Carlile for the Oklahoma County seat six years earlier. Berry stormed out of the meeting, announcing that he would not participate in conferences attended by Welch. A reporter for the *Oklahoma City Times* heard about the confrontation and wrote about the incident.[19]

On the evening of January 12, eight days after the incident with Welch, Berry received a telephone call at his home from U.S. district judge Stephen Chandler, the eccentric jurist who had heard the Selected Investments bankruptcy case and had listened to the preposterous Pierre Laval testimony from Hugh Carroll. Chandler, whom Berry considered an acquaintance but by no means a friend, asked Berry to come immediately to Chandler's home in northwest Oklahoma City. When Berry arrived, he found a nervous Chandler waiting for him. Upon Berry's entering the residence, Chandler, known for being obsessed with personal security, bolted several locks, then handed Berry a copy of the eighty-four-page statement N. S. Corn had given to U.S. Attorney B. Andrew Potter and Oklahoma County Attorney James Harrod the previous month. Although the statement's existence had become public knowledge, its contents had remained undisclosed. Chandler did not explain where he had received a copy of Corn's statement, but it was obvious to Berry that it was indeed from Corn. Corn's statement included his involvement with O. A. Cargill, his solicitation of the bribe in the *Selected Investments* appeal, and his acceptance of a bribe in *Marshall v. Amos*. He also described his sharing the bribe money with Welch and Justice N. B. Johnson, who was still sitting on the court and whose name had not yet been linked to the scandal.

After Berry read and digested Corn's claim, Chandler asked Berry what he intended to do with the statement. Berry responded with the obvious, asking the judge why Chandler himself couldn't do something. Chandler told Berry that as a federal judge his hands were tied; the federal court had no jurisdiction, and any action would have to come from the state courts. This explanation was nonsense. Not only did the federal courts have jurisdiction over the scandal, the federal courts had been asserting that jurisdiction all along; Welch and Corn had each been convicted in federal court of evading federal income taxes. The prosecutors, most of whom were federal employees, had taken Corn's statement at a federal correctional facility from a federal prisoner.[20]

A question not addressed by Justice Berry in his memoir on the scandal is how and why Chandler obtained the statement in the first place. It was extraordinary that a sitting judge had obtained, much less accepted, a sensitive document from a prosecutor's file. Chandler was no friend of prosecutors, and whoever leaked the statement to him had done so surreptitiously and in violation of government policy. Although deciphering the unusual mind of Stephen Chandler is a difficult task, it seems likely that he passed the statement on to Berry in order to remain anonymous and to protect the source of the document. It also seems logical that he picked Berry because of Berry's well-publicized antipathy toward Welch.

Having been handed a smoking gun, Berry now debated what to do. He decided that if the statement were to be made public, the person releasing it must be someone who would not be susceptible to a libel suit.[21] This led Berry to the legislature, whose members were legally immune from liability for any statement made on the floor during a legislative session. After the first legislator failed to return his calls, he turned to G. T. Blankenship, a Republican legislator-attorney from Oklahoma City. Berry called Blankenship and asked him to come to his home. Blankenship read the statement; astounded and horrified, Blankenship immediately agreed to announce its existence on the House floor and to summarize its contents.[22]

On Thursday, January 21, only nine days after Berry's startling conversation with Chandler and immediately after the House Rules Committee had announced a delay in the Welch impeachment investigation, Blankenship rose and asked to address the House. He then made the landmark speech described in this book's first pages. Blankenship laid his career on the line by describing Corn's statement to the authorities, the involvement of Welch and Johnson, the corruption in the *Selected Investments* decision, and the corrupt influence of Cargill, to whom Blankenship referred as "Mister X."

By "letting the genie out of the bottle," as Justice Berry later put it, Blankenship angered the Democratic leadership. He also infuriated prosecutors. Oklahoma County Attorney Curtis Harris, who had held the statement only since assuming office from Harrod on January 4, called Blankenship a "yellow belly," chiding Blankenship for his referral to Cargill as "Mister X," not naming Cargill publicly. U.S. Attorney B. Andrew Potter also criticized Blankenship, citing the "inordinate curiosity" of "certain people" and claimed Blankenship had jeopardized the investigation.[23] Corn had given his statement only the previous month, so law enforcement authorities had indeed had little time to verify it. Harris himself had been in office for less than a month, having succeeded James Harrod. Corn had provided the first hard evidence against N. B. Johnson. In order to prosecute Johnson successfully, testimony coming from a questionable source like Corn would have to be corroborated and supported with documentary evidence. This would take time, so the prosecutors' reluctance to have the evidence enter the public realm so quickly is understandable.

On the other hand, Oklahoma was faced with the shocking situation of having one former justice making claims of bribery and a second justice, now a convicted felon and named bribery suspect, still on the bench. An allegation of bribery against Justice Johnson, also still in office, had been made by Corn. The fact that Corn had made a statement was already in the public realm; the only question was the statement's contents. On the whole, it was probably unrealistic for Potter, Harrod, and Harris to expect to be able to keep Corn's sensational confession confidential. A political emergency existed: two sitting Supreme Court justices were accused by a former justice of accepting bribes. Blankenship and Berry would have been derelict not to bring the facts to public attention.

On the day after Blankenship's speech, Chief Justice W. H. Blackbird called a meeting of the Supreme Court. All of the justices, including Welch and Johnson, attended. Welch, whose tax returns were already in the public record in his criminal case, for some reason objected to Berry's suggestion that all justices release their income tax returns. Justice Johnson seemed stunned, shaking his head and cursing an unnamed person. It was unclear to Berry whether Johnson was referring to Corn or Blankenship.[24] Publicly, Johnson denied the charge, calling it "false, positively false."[25]

On February 15, a federal grand jury, which had listened to Cargill's testimony ten months previously, indicted him on three counts of perjury, ending Blankenship's poorly kept secret of the identity of Mr. X. Cargill's indictment spelled out the incidents in which he had allegedly lied. Cargill had told the grand jury that he did not know where the unexplained $150,000 Selected Investments expenditure had gone, and that he had no idea Pierre Laval was a fictional person. When asked whether he had any financial transactions with any member of the Supreme Court, Cargill had coyly replied, "None that I know of at all."[26] By their indictment of Cargill, the grand jurors had shown their disbelief of all of these statements. On February 19 Cargill appeared for his initial hearing in front of Judge Harper. Astonishingly, even after all that had occurred, Cargill had not hired a lawyer, so his son and law partner Buck represented him at the initial hearing.[27]

Cargill should never have allowed himself to be in such legal peril. Even in April 1964 he had known he was required to appear before a federal grand jury. He would have either known or suspected that his former client Hugh Carroll was cooperating with the government. He knew that he, Corn, and Welch were suspects. An objective lawyer with even minimal criminal law experience, given this situation, would have advised his client to take advantage of the Fifth Amendment. Had Cargill asserted his Fifth Amendment privilege, he would not have been required to testify and thus would not have committed perjury. As a former prosecutor and experienced criminal defense attorney, Cargill would have known this. Even talented attorneys are subject to error, though, when it comes to their own legal problems; Cargill's hubris and overconfidence had worked to his disadvantage.

On February 22, Oklahoma County attorney Curtis Harris announced a state grand jury investigation into the activities of the Supreme Court, issuing subpoenas for Carroll, Corn, various Cargill associates, former justice and attorney Wayne Bayless, and nearly everyone involved in *Marshall v. Amos*. Why another investigation was necessary was difficult to understand, but this was the first official law enforcement inquiry since Corn's statement had become public knowledge. At Harris's recommendation, the district court gave immunity from prosecution to Carroll and Corn, both of whom testified on February 25.[28]

Impeachment Proceedings

Meanwhile, legislative efforts to impeach Justices Welch and Johnson were gathering steam. On March 10 Welch testified for four hours in an overcrowded conference room before the House Impeachment Committee, the first time he had told his story in public. Appearing confident, Welch emphatically denied taking bribes from anyone. He refuted Corn's statement, stating simply that Corn was a "sick man" who must have wanted "out of that place [prison] in the worst sort of way." Welch engaged in a double-talking sparring match with Representative Burke Mordy of Ardmore regarding Welch's willingness to take a polygraph test. Welch repeatedly insisted he would take only a polygraph approved for use in the court, knowing that in fact the result of polygraphs were not admissible in court.[29] Welch did offer to resign if his conviction were affirmed by the Tenth Circuit Court of Appeals, an empty offer since Welch would then be headed to prison.[30]

On March 16 the committee went to the home of R. O. Ingle, who had been Johnson's legal assistant for twelve years. Ingle, who was suffering from a serious respiratory illness and awaiting admission to a hospital, testified while wearing his bathrobe and lying on a sofa. Ingle claimed in 1956 he saw Pat O'Bryan, then the attorney for Selected Investments, and another man, possibly Hugh Carroll, enter Johnson's office. After the conversation ended, according to Ingle, Johnson, who appeared to have been drinking, placed a brief on Ingle's desk and suggested the case be reversed. Generally, Ingle spoke highly of Johnson but did claim he was too easily influenced by his friends, especially Earl Welch.[31]

It is hard to know what to think of Ingle's testimony. His statement was the only direct link between Johnson and Selected Investments; all other testimony clearly showed the bribes were handled strictly between Hugh Carroll and N. S. Corn. Ingle, a native of Spiro in Welch's eastern Oklahoma district, had unsuccessfully run against Welch three years earlier, and had no great regard for him.³² However, Ingle obviously liked Johnson, had worked for him for twelve years, and had no apparent reason to harm him. The ailing Ingle did not testify at Johnson's impeachment trial before the State Senate the next month, so the accuracy of Ingle's story was therefore never verified or tested in court.

Cargill finally employed flamboyant criminal defense attorney Percy Foreman from Houston. Appearing by telegram, Foreman predictably and appropriately instructed his client to invoke the Fifth Amendment before the House Impeachment Committee. Cargill's side of the story therefore went temporarily untold.

The House Investigations Committee was set to recommend impeachment against both Welch and Johnson on the afternoon of March 21. That morning Earl Welch finally resigned his post on the Oklahoma Supreme Court, submitting a lengthy, self-serving letter to Governor Bellmon. The resignation made Welch's impeachment moot. The Investigations Committee recommended Justice Johnson's impeachment and outlined for the record the evidence it had gathered against Welch prior to Welch's resignation.³³ On March 24, the House of Representatives, by votes of 90-6 and 88-8, voted to impeach Johnson on two counts.

The articles of impeachment accused Johnson of taking a seventy-five-hundred-dollar bribe in the *Selected Investments* case and a twenty-five-hundred-dollar bribe in *Oklahoma Company v. O'Neil*, the oil and gas case that involved Cargill's daughter and son-in-law. The other cases in which the parties suspected corruption were not mentioned. Johnson, who still had not retained a lawyer, immediately moved to suspend himself. Although Johnson's authority to suspend himself seemed doubtful, the Senate accepted his offer and formally suspended Johnson from office pending his impeachment trial.³⁴ Two days later the Oklahoma County grand jury indicted Cargill, Welch, and Johnson in state district court, charging them with bribery. Cargill took advantage of his initial hearing on the bribery charge to proclaim his innocence and call the grand jury a "star chamber."³⁵

In the meantime, the Senate, which had never expected to be sitting as a court of impeachment, took its job very seriously. Each senator solemnly raised his right hand and swore to perform his duty as a member of the court. The Senate named Roy Grantham, an attorney-legislator from Ponca City, as the trial's presiding officer and enacted rules for the impeachment proceedings, by and large adopting Oklahoma's district court rules on the admissibility of evidence. After considerable debate the senators decided to allow television into the chamber, as long as the lights did not interfere with the dignity of the proceedings. Under the rules, the Senate as a body had the right to overrule the chair on evidentiary issues.[36]

No one had much experience in the matter of impeachments, although this had not been the case in previous generations. The first years after Oklahoma's 1907 statehood had seen fifteen impeachment trials. Four early-statehood officeholders, including two governors, had been removed from office. The chaotic year of 1929 alone saw efforts to impeach six officials, including Governor Henry S. Johnston, four members of the Supreme Court, and the president of the state board of agriculture. While the four justices and the board president had either had their cases dismissed or been acquitted, Johnston had been convicted and removed.[37] After the bloodletting of 1929, however, public and legislative enthusiasm for impeachment had dwindled. Since that year, only one serious effort at impeachment, an unsuccessful 1945 attempt to remove the state superintendent of schools, occurred.[38]

Like Cargill, N. B. Johnson waited until the last minute to hire an attorney. Even after Corn's conviction and statement, the grand juries, Blankenship's speech on the House floor, the impeachment committee, and Carroll's testimony, Johnson had hidden his head in the sand. Only three days before his first mandatory appearance before the Senate did Johnson finally hire attorneys: George Bingaman from Purcell, a former justice, and Fred Green from Sallisaw, a respected lawyer active in Democratic politics.[39] Green and Bingaman would be opposed by the House-appointed members of the Board of Managers: Representatives Lou Allard of Drumright, Burke G. Mordy of Ardmore, James W. Connor of Bartlesville, Phil Smalley of Norman, and Nathan S. Sherman of Oklahoma City. After appearing before the Senate and entering his plea of not guilty, Johnson told the press, "The most important thing is to clear my name." At Green's request, the trial was continued until May 6.[40]

Like Corn, Welch, and Cargill, Napoleon Bonaparte Johnson, a member of the Cherokee Nation, was a product of the frontier. Even more than his fellow conspirators, Johnson seemed to symbolize the American Dream. Born in 1891 Johnson moved in early childhood from his father's home in Locust Grove—a mountainous, wooded settlement with only Cherokee cabins and few white people present—to the home of his mother's family in present-day southern Oklahoma. Since there were no public schools in the Chickasaw

Nation, Johnson attended a Presbyterian school for underprivileged children in Anadarko. He graduated from the ninth grade, went into the navy for a short time, then attended college. After a few years working for the U.S. Indian Service, he decided to become a lawyer, attended law school in Tennessee, and was admitted to the Oklahoma bar in 1922.[41]

Johnson and his family settled in Claremore, where he worked as a prosecutor and practiced law. In 1934 Johnson was elected district judge, a position he held for fourteen years. Johnson became very active in Native American affairs, serving on various boards supporting Native American interests. In 1948, supported by Senator Elmer Thomas and Governor Robert S. Kerr, he was a serious candidate for appointment as U.S. commissioner of Indian affairs.[42] When President Truman eventually named another candidate to the post, Johnson successfully ran for the Oklahoma Supreme Court against incumbent Wayne Bayless.[43] Seventeen years later, Justice Johnson, who had risen from poverty and a mission boarding school to the Supreme Court of his native state and a national leadership role among Native American people, now found himself the respondent in an impeachment trial before the Oklahoma State Senate.

The Senate constituted a unique group of jurors. Approximately half of them were lawyers, some with years of courtroom experience.[44] All were men. One, E. Melvin Porter of Oklahoma City, was African American.[45] By virtue of their being in the Senate, all had achieved high office, were competitive, and were politically astute. All felt a responsibility to their constituents and knew they would have to explain their votes. Most would have had at least a casual acquaintance with Justice Johnson, who had worked for years in the state capitol, the same building that housed the Senate. Under the impeachment rules, senators could submit proposed questions to the presiding officer, who, if he approved of the question, would relay it.

Hugh Carroll was the prosecution's first significant witness. Carroll related his shared northwestern Oklahoma background with Corn, the potentially disastrous effect the Oklahoma Tax Commission ruling would have had on his company, his dinner with Corn in which they made the arrangement for a $150,000 bribe, the favorable ruling, and his eventual payment of the money to Corn. In his cross-examination, Bingaman implied that Carroll subsidized Corn's small loan company in the 1940s, inquired about the fictitious Pierre Laval testimony in bankruptcy court, and alluded to Carroll's extravagant withdrawals from his various companies. Bingaman was unable to cause Carroll significant damage, although he did point out Carroll's previous contradictory stories.[46]

Corn, who appeared before the Senate tieless and somewhat disheveled, nevertheless did Johnson considerable harm. Under questioning from Representative Burke Mordy from Ardmore, Corn calmly relayed the stories of the briberies in *Selected Investments* and *Oklahoma Company v. O'Neil*. He outlined his bribery proposals with both Welch and Johnson, his delivery of bribe money to each of them at their offices in the capitol, and Johnson's counting the money. Grantham, the presiding officer, severely limited Bingaman's cross-examination of the witness, but Bingaman was able to establish Corn's colon cancer at the time of the bribes, his hostility toward O. A. Cargill, and his insistence on immunity from prosecution at Welch's tax evasion trial. Corn also admitted he had told Floyd Rheam, who had accepted Corn's letter of resignation from the bar, that no other justices had taken a bribe. Corn did point out that Welch was in his home and was able to overhear his conversation with Rheam.

The questions from the senators primarily involved why Corn had thought Welch and Johnson could be bribed. Corn's answers to these questions were evasive, and the Senate voted not to force the witness to be more specific. Corn originally said his reasons for approaching the two justices would be based on hearsay, but he eventually testified he based his feeling on his experience in *Marshall v. Amos*.[47]

As in the cases of Corn and Welch, Johnson's financial records proved to be his undoing. Johnson had banked at two banks in Claremore and had accounts and a safety deposit box at Citizens National Bank (earlier Citizens State) in Oklahoma City. Johnson's Oklahoma City banker testified Johnson entered his safety deposit box eleven times between December 1959 and March 1962. He also purchased about $6,900 in cashier's checks, which he used to pay various expenses, including his $89.51-per-month house payment and loans at the Claremore banks.[48]

On May 10, the most important witness of the trial, Johnson himself, began his testimony. In Bingaman's direct examination of his client, Bingaman went into considerable detail about Johnson's background, his professional awards, and his success as an attorney. Bingaman largely avoided the elephant in the room: his client's votes in *Selected Investments* and *Oklahoma Company v. O'Neil*. Instead, he merely asked, without elaboration, whether Johnson had taken bribes from Corn on the two cases. Johnson simply said, "That testimony was false."⁴⁹ Bingaman's strategy was dangerous: the only reason for the trial was to determine whether Johnson had accepted bribes from Corn. Bingaman's failure to elicit Johnson's side of the story from his client left the door open to force the witness to tell it in unfriendly and unsympathetic cross-examination.

Under Representative James W. Connor's questioning, Johnson denied directing his legal assistant, R. O. Ingle, to draft an opinion reversing the trial court in the *Selected Investments* case. Connor forced Johnson to admit having asked several friends to contact their senators on his behalf before the impeachment trial, with the justice explaining that all he wanted was a "fair deal."⁵⁰ Johnson testified he had kept large amounts of cash, often about $2,000, hidden at his home, which he claimed to have obtained from cashing routine checks and keeping leftover money. Johnson admitted to opening a safety deposit box at his Oklahoma City bank on June 19, 1957, and entering the box on five separate occasions that same year. Connor was able to prove Johnson purchased nineteen cashier's checks totaling $3,400 on the same dates he entered the box. Johnson stopped this practice after April 1961, when he received a letter from Harlan Grimes accusing him of bribery in the *Selected Investments* decision.⁵¹

In total, between July 1956 and March 1962, Johnson bought cashier's checks totaling $6,909.89 from Citizens National Bank of Oklahoma City, the same bank in which he had the safety deposit box. This established the prosecution's argument that Johnson put the $7,500 *Selected Investment* bribe in the box, removing cash and buying cashier's checks when he needed the money. He made seventeen house payments in cash.

Johnson had no valid explanation for his frequent entries into the box, where he admitted keeping about eight hundred dollars in cash.⁵² Justice Johnson simply could not account for his financial expenditures and had no valid or comprehensible explanation for the source of the money. Questions from senators repeatedly asked Johnson to explain the financial discrepancy, but Johnson did not provide one.⁵³ By failing to provide a reasonable hypothesis other than guilt, Johnson had harmed his own case.

On May 13, after seven days of trial and closing arguments, the Senate went into private session to discuss the evidence.⁵⁴ After four hours behind closed doors, Grantham called for a vote, and the clerk began to call the roll, which was conducted in alphabetical order. Under the rules, the prosecution was required to obtain a two-thirds majority in the Senate in order to remove

Justice Johnson from office. With three votes left, the count stood at 29 to 15 in favor of conviction; unless all three of the remaining senators voted to convict, Johnson would be acquitted. Senators Al Terrill from Lawton, G. W. Williams from Gore, and John Young from Sapulpa all voted in favor of conviction; Johnson had been removed from office by one vote. The vote on the now superfluous second count, the bribe in *Oklahoma Company v. O'Neil*, was identical. Johnson became the first Oklahoma Supreme Court justice to be removed from office.[55]

More than a half-century later, the case against N. B. Johnson appears to be overwhelming. Corn, who had no particular grudge against Johnson, testified he had personally bribed Johnson and handed him the money on both occasions. Hugh Carroll confirmed most of Corn's story, although he had never dealt directly with Johnson. Johnson's own financial records proved he had outspent his income, hoarded inordinate amounts of cash, and although he had a checking account, often visited his safety deposit box and inexplicably paid his bills with cashier's checks or cash. Both direct and circumstantial evidence pointed to Johnson's guilt, and very little evidence exonerating him had been presented.

Nevertheless, Johnson still received fifteen votes for acquittal. Of the fifteen, all but Richard Romang of Enid were Democrats. All four of the senators from overwhelmingly Democratic southeastern Oklahoma voted to exonerate Johnson.[56] Clem McSpadden, the powerful president pro tempore of the Senate, was from Johnson's hometown of Claremore and supported Johnson. E. Melvin Porter of Oklahoma City, the first African American to serve in the Senate, voted for acquittal, as did Charles Pope from Tulsa. The other eight senators from Oklahoma County and six from Tulsa County voted to convict.[57] It is therefore reasonable to conclude that if the 1965 legislature had not been reapportioned and had remained disproportionately rural, the result may have been different for N. B. Johnson.

On July 22, having been delayed by congressional redistricting and the Johnson trial, the second-longest legislative session in Oklahoma history finally limped to a close. Although it was criticized for its slow and cumbersome work, the session generally received good marks. In the legal world, the legislature had removed Welch and Johnson and replaced the county attorneys with a district attorney system. It failed, however, to address the subject of judicial reform, including justices of the peace.[58] The next legislature and next governor would be forced to deal with that issue.

The O. A. Cargill Perjury Trial

The O. A. Cargill perjury trial began on June 1, 1965, before Judge Harper. Percy Foreman, the nationally known, flamboyant criminal defense attorney representing Cargill, immediately irritated Judge Harper, alluding to his busy schedule and telling the judge at an April 30 pretrial hearing that he "to this good hour" had not devoted any time to Cargill's case and had filed "canned motions" prepared by his secretary. Harper expressed surprise that a lawyer would admit to filing boilerplate motions.[59] This foreshadowed what was to come, as Harper and Foreman would clash throughout the trial.

Cargill had been charged with three counts of perjury; the grand jury claimed he had lied when he denied knowing anything about the Selected Investments bribe, when he denied in bankruptcy court authoring the phony Pierre Laval story, and when he denied having financial dealings with any Supreme Court justices.[60] After the jury was selected, Harper immediately ordered the jurors sequestered in an Oklahoma City hotel, where they were placed under armed guard, without access to telephones, radios, or televisions.[61]

Hugh Carroll became the prosecution's first significant witness. Carroll related his story of meeting Cargill at Corn's insistence in the days before his bankruptcy hearing in March 1958. Carroll described his conspiracy with Corn, his payment of the $150,000, Cargill's comment that he could have bribed the judges for less money, and Carroll's obvious reluctance to reveal where the $200,000 Selected Investments expenditure had gone. Carroll testified that he had planned to invoke the Fifth Amendment when asked about the $200,000, but Cargill persuaded him to testify to the Pierre Laval story instead, which Cargill apparently made up on the spot after learning Carroll had a cabin in Canada.[62] Carroll told the jury he finally told the truth to federal and state authorities after receiving immunity from prosecution in April 1964.

On cross-examination George Miskovsky, a former senator assisting in Cargill's defense, repeatedly quizzed Carroll on his memory but was unable to shake Carroll's basic story of what had happened seven years previously. However, Miskovsky did establish that Carroll had told others he needed money to buy stock in Selected Investments and to pay lobbyists to resist measures pending in the legislature that were unfavorable to the company. Carroll's wife, Julia, testified as well, verifying her husband's testimony about Cargill's invention of Pierre Laval and her expressing her disapproval of Cargill, his forceful and overbearing manner, and his invention of such a preposterous lie.[63]

Corn began his testimony on June 4. He described his long and corrupt relationship with Cargill, his accepting small amounts of money over the years from Cargill, Cargill's calls telling him to "get his pencil out," and his belief that Cargill had similar relationships with other justices. Corn told the jury about his hiding ninety-seven thousand dollars in his golf shoes in his lockers, in fruit jars in his backyard, and in filing cabinets. He admitted that when Carroll asked for the return of the money after the company went into receivership, he only returned thirty-three thousand dollars, even though he still had more of the bribe money left. Corn also testified that he received four thousand dollars from Cargill in *Marshall v. Amos,* the Cleveland County oil and gas case, and twenty-five hundred dollars in *Oklahoma Company v. O'Neil,* the case involving Cargill's daughter and son-in-law. He admitted that because of his previous payments from Cargill, he would have voted Cargill's way regardless of the extra bribes. Corn testified that Cargill told him he had "taken care of" the other justices in *Marshall v. Amos.*[64] He then described his bitter break with Cargill over Corn's tax troubles in February 1961.[65]

In his lengthy and detailed cross-examination, Foreman meticulously pointed out many cases in which Corn had voted against Cargill's clients. According to Foreman, of a dozen cases involving Cargill that he had lost, Corn did not vote in five, voted against Cargill in four, and authored the opinion against him in yet another case. Corn explained that Cargill often had arrangements with opposing attorneys to lose cases, and that sometimes Cargill did not call him at all. Foreman also noted that Corn, while he was still incarcerated in Springfield, received immunity from further federal prosecution from Acting Attorney General Nicholas D. Katzenbach as well as an oral immunity promise from Oklahoma County attorney James Harrod.[66] Toward the end of testimony, Corn turned toward the judge and said, "I violated my oath and I ruined myself. . . . I ruined myself completely, disgraced my family, disappointed my friends. . . . The only thing to do now is to come in and tell the truth, and that's what I'm doing."[67]

H. G. Marshall, the former Oklahoma City oilman at the center of *Marshall v. Amos,* related his background with Cargill, whom he had known since 1928. Marshall had also been a friend of Cargill's daughter and son-in-law and had talked with Cargill about his case. Although Cargill had done no legal work on Marshall's case, Cargill, according to Marshall, told him he had a "dangerous lawsuit," and that he could guarantee a win "with the boys on the hill" for thirty thousand dollars. Titus Haffa, Marshall's Chicago colleague, then prepared a letter guaranteeing Cargill thirty thousand dollars upon reversal of the case.

On cross-examination Foreman was able to harm Marshall's credibility considerably, exposing him as a prevaricating, profane man with more than forty judgments against him and a history of driving under the influence and bogus check prosecutions. Foreman forced Marshall to admit he had told Ardmore attorney Earl Grey, who was investigating the matter for the Oklahoma Bar Association, that he hired Cargill solely for his legal ability. Foreman also noted contradictory stories Marshall had told to private investigators and mentioned other cases in which Cargill had represented Marshall, implying the thirty thousand dollars was for past services, not a bribe.[68] Titus Haffa followed Marshall to the stand; Haffa did so badly that Harper warned him of the penalties for perjury.[69]

Foreman began the defense case with Merle Zwifel, who had been convicted of mail fraud and been assigned to Carroll's cottage at the federal penitentiary in Seagoville, Texas. Zwifel testified that Carroll had been extremely worried about money and about being charged in state district court. Carroll allegedly told Zwifel he had $150,000 stashed in a secret location near his cabin in Canada. The next day Cargill's wife testified, recalling the visit Hugh and Julia Carroll had made to their ranch prior to the bankruptcy hearing in March 1958. She remembered driving with the Carrolls to see the ranch's buffalo but denied any discussion of Pierre Laval.[70] Foreman then presented several justices, as well as attorneys who had prevailed in cases against Cargill; all denied having any financial dealings with him.

It now became Cargill's turn to testify. Appearing nervous initially, Cargill related his biography to the jury, telling them of his background in Arkansas, his migration to Oklahoma, his becoming an attorney and mayor of Oklahoma City, his religious work, the death of his daughter, and his successful law practice. With the exception of small campaign contributions, Cargill denied any financial dealings with Justice Corn or any other member of the court. He denied receiving twenty-five hundred dollars from Corn for securing Lon Carlile's vote in the *Selected Investments* case and insisted the thirty thousand dollars he received from Haffa was for his earlier representation of Haffa and Marshall in a Noble County case.

On the subject of *Selected Investments*, Cargill admitted meeting the Carrolls at his home but denied concocting the Pierre Laval story. Cargill testified he had anticipated receiving a continuance from "Steve" (Judge Chandler) and was stunned when the judge denied his request. He said he heard the name "Pierre Laval" for the first time in court. As to N. S. Corn, Cargill claimed he had not been particularly cordial with Corn since the early 1940s, when Cargill backed Corn's rival Ben Arnold for chief justice.[71] Cargill said he had offended Corn by suing Corn's small loan companies in the 1940s.[72] He denied meeting Corn on the street with money, denied ever being in Corn's office at the capitol, denied underwriting Corn's campaigns, and denied telling Corn to "grab your pencil."[73]

In his cross-examination of Cargill, Assistant U.S. Attorney David Kline established Cargill's familiarity with the business affairs of Selected Investments at the bankruptcy court hearing. He also pointed out that Hugh Carroll, Julia Carroll, and N. S. Corn gave similar testimony. According to Cargill, Hugh Carroll had actually employed Ned Looney to represent him but for some reason made the twenty-five-thousand-dollar check to Cargill. Kline established the lack of logic of receiving a twenty-five-thousand-dollar fee from Carroll, then learning about Pierre Laval for the first time in the courtroom.[74]

In rebuttal, the prosecution called James Nance, a former legislator and publisher from Purcell, who testified that Cargill offered him ten thousand dollars to obtain Justice Floyd Jackson's vote on the Meadors will case. Nance admitted, however, that he did not share this information with Justice Jackson for two or three years. The government also called Laura Fleming, who accused Cargill of trying to coerce her into selling him an oil and gas lease on favorable terms, claiming he had the Supreme Court fixed against her.[75]

After lengthy closing arguments, in which Foreman attacked the credibility of government witnesses, the case went to the jury. After nine hours of deliberation, the jury returned its verdict at 1 A.M.: guilty on all counts. Cargill ironically told the press he had been "convicted on perjured testimony." The next month Harper sentenced Cargill to five years imprisonment and a three-thousand-dollar fine. As he had done with Corn, he ordered him to be immediately eligible for parole.

The year of 1965 exposed the shocking size and breadth of the Oklahoma judicial scandal. It was now known that certain justices of the Oklahoma Supreme Court had been receiving bribes for many years. Corn, Welch, and Cargill had been convicted, and Johnson had been removed from office. All the primary actors were to pass their last years in disgrace. While the extent of the corruption had become public knowledge, nothing had been done to prevent something like this from reoccurring. The Oklahoma body politic would deal with this problem in the next two years.

5
The Fall of McCarty, the Sneed Plan, and the Election of 1966

Since 1961, Speaker J. D. McCarty had ruled the Oklahoma House of Representatives with an iron hand. Tough, smart, and energetic, he almost single-handedly determined the passage or failure of legislation. A generation later, a still-frustrated Henry Bellmon described his feelings about Speaker McCarty, calling him the "Oklahoma prototype of the worst kind of politician. . . . As Speaker of the House, he became loud, fat, power-mad, and heavy-handed in his dealing with those over whom he could exert either influence or authority." According to Bellmon, McCarty's control over the House "was absolute. Anytime he took the rostrum and pointed his thumb upward, the matter under consideration passed with a huge majority. Anytime he made the opposite gesture, the measure failed."[1] Little or nothing in Oklahoma's state government took place without McCarty's approval.

Although he represented an Oklahoma City district, McCarty had the ability to "think rural," which meant being able to protect the members of his rural Democratic caucus.[2] McCarty generally allied himself with Democratic, conservative legislators, many of whom came from the southern half of the state. He tended to see issues, including judicial reform, along party lines and dragged his feet on proposals that changed the status quo. The legislature's huge Democratic majority allowed him to avoid accountability from the questioning of a strong minority party. As judicially mandated reapportionment changed the legislature's demographics to allow greater urban participation, McCarty remained loyal to his rural, conservative power base.

In late 1964 and early 1965 McCarty considered running for governor or a seat on the Corporation Commission. He also considered abandoning politics altogether and entering private business full-time. Eventually, he decided instead to run for a fourth term as Speaker of the House. Even before he definitely made up his mind whether to seek to retain his Speaker's post, he had pledges of seventy votes, well more than he needed for reelection.[3]

The first rumblings of trouble for McCarty came in September 1964. Muriel Luther (Jack) Woosley, a pilot with a minor criminal history, claimed to have flown two legislators, not yet identified as McCarty and Senate president pro tempore Everett Collins, to Memphis. Woosley said that a lawyer and a state crime bureau agent also made the trip, which was designed to arrange bribes for the legislators to sponsor a bill legalizing dog tracks in Oklahoma. Woosley told the story to his next-door neighbor, who was an assistant county attorney, who arranged for Woosley to meet with County Attorney James Harrod. When Harrod did not react with the speed Woosley thought appropriate, Woosley contacted the newly founded *Oklahoma Journal*, a daily newspaper begun by millionaire Midwest City developer Bill Atkinson, who blamed the *Daily Oklahoman* and *Oklahoma City Times* for his 1962 gubernatorial loss to Bellmon and had started a competing daily paper.

The *Journal* printed the story but did not name any names, leaving the reader to guess the respective identities of the parties.[4] After the story came out, the *Daily Oklahoman* identified Woosley as the complainant, insinuated that Woosley had ruined the investigation by failing to cooperate with Harrod, and included Woosley's arrest record. The matter might have died on the vine, but the next day Woosley sued the *Oklahoman* for $2 million, claiming the article had defamed him.[5] Woosley's lawsuit, even though it was frivolous, forced the newspaper to defend itself in court and to inquire into Woosley's allegations. The discovery process in the litigation would help lead to the end of McCarty's political career.

The attorneys for the *Oklahoman* sent written inquiries to Woosley's lawyer. After normal courthouse business hours on July 28, 1965, the last permissible day to respond, Woosley's lawyers filed their client's responses to the newspaper's questions. Woosley claimed under oath that in late 1960 he had flown Whit Pate, a former Howard Edmondson aide and an attorney practicing in Poteau and Oklahoma City, and Forest Castle, a former head of the Oklahoma Crime Bureau, to Memphis. The trip's purpose was for Pate to pick up thirty thousand dollars from Tennessee racing interests, who were seeking to legalize horse and dog racing in Oklahoma. After the group returned to Oklahoma, Pate called McCarty and Collins, who met Pate in Pate's hotel room. Pate then delivered ten thousand dollars each to McCarty and Collins, kept five thousand dollars for himself, and paid the other five thousand dollars to Castle.

According to Woosley, in January 1961 Pate returned to Memphis, this time by commercial plane and without Woosley. Pate then reportedly returned with another thirty thousand dollars. After his return to Oklahoma, Pate met McCarty and Collins at the Turner Turnpike gate, where McCarty took ten thousand dollars, Collins took ten thousand dollars, and Pate kept the other ten thousand dollars, later giving five thousand dollars to Castle.

Woosley also claimed he had learned that an individual named Bob Lewis had paid McCarty five thousand dollars to kill the horse racing and dog racing legislation, with a promise of another forty-five thousand dollars to the speaker when the bill was finally dead. When he was asked about this, McCarty had reportedly told Pate he had indeed taken the five thousand dollars from the opponents of racing. McCarty allegedly had said that this was simply an easy way to make five thousand dollars, and that Pate and the others had nothing to worry about.[6]

Woosley's claim was indeed alarming. Assuming the truth of what Woosley was saying, the Speaker of the House of Representatives and the president pro tempore of the Senate had accepted twenty thousand dollars each to influence the passage of important legislation. McCarty had also accepted an additional five thousand dollars, with the promise of forty-five thousand dollars more to kill that same legislation, thus accepting large bribes from both sides of the issue.[7] However, Woosley's story had significant problems. First, even according to Woosley, he had seen very few of the events firsthand. He had flown the plane to Memphis with Pate and Castle and returned with the money. He had little or no interaction with McCarty and Collins; almost all of his information had come from Pate. Moreover, Woosley had little credibility. He admitted misleading Harrod about the source of the bribe money, telling the county attorney the money came from dog breeders, not gamblers.[8] It was no wonder that Harrod had hesitated to file a criminal case based primarily on Woosley. If prosecutors were to prove a bribery case against McCarty and Collins, the information would have to come from Pate and Castle.

Pate was having a highly public, if not overly productive, career. After graduating from law school at the University of Arkansas, Pate began practicing law in Heavener. He campaigned for the 1958 election of Governor J. Howard Edmondson and became the governor's first legal counsel after Edmondson's inauguration. Pate, whose political ties were to the conservative forces in southeastern Oklahoma, was a poor fit in Edmondson's office, and he resigned after three months.⁹ Pate then opened a law office in Oklahoma City and was a law partner of former governor Johnston Murray for a few months in 1960.¹⁰ Pate tried elective politics, running unsuccessfully for a seat on the Corporation Commission in 1960 and again in 1962.¹¹ He also acquired a reputation for mercurial conduct; as an acting county judge in Leflore County, he once ordered his own brother Pat, the Leflore County attorney, to jail for five days.¹²

Pate told a bar investigating committee that he and Senator Gene Stipe had split a $150,000 bribe from industrial firms wanting inside information on a water pipeline being built between Oklahoma City and Lake Atoka, calling the day they received the money "the day we shot the elephant."¹³ Weeks later, he signed an affidavit denying that very claim. In March 1965, in trouble with the Oklahoma Bar Association (OBA) as a result of his contradictory testimony, Pate ignored a subpoena from the OBA committee investigating his fitness to practice law.¹⁴

In addition to his problems with the bar, Pate had other issues. Constantly in debt, he was often sued by his creditors. He also probably was impaired by drugs. In 1970 he sued a New Jersey drug manufacturer, claiming an arthritis drug had caused him to behave bizarrely. Among other things, he claimed he could not remember why he left the employ of Governor Edmondson and could barely remember the events of 1966.¹⁵ Whit Pate, in short, was unreliable and not credible.

The *Oklahoman* story about the dog racing bribery claim caused public outrage and demands for an investigation into the conduct of McCarty and Collins. Curtis Harris, the Oklahoma County district attorney, announced that his office would investigate the case and, if necessary, request that a grand jury be called.¹⁶ Within a few days two Oklahoma City women, asking help only from their friends and neighbors, had obtained the necessary number of signatures to authorize a grand jury. Oklahoma City radio station KTOK joined the drive for signatures, suggesting its listeners to visit the station to sign the petition.¹⁷

The grand jury began to investigate the McCarty issue on November 8, 1965, with the first subpoenaed witness being Whit Pate. Curtis Harris, the prosecutor, wanted to ask Pate about an affidavit he had given a reporter confirming the payoffs, then retracted with another affidavit prepared by an Oklahoma City lawyer representing McCarty's interests denying the events had ever occurred. Harris had evidence that the lawyer obtaining Pate's second affidavit paid Pate twenty-five hundred dollars in exchange for his signing the document.

Pate could not possibly reconcile his stories. He refused to testify, invoking his Fifth Amendment privilege against self-incrimination. Judge Jo Ann McInnis, at Harris's request, granted Pate immunity from prosecution.[18] Pate, despite being granted immunity and being ordered to testify, still refused to do so. McInnis ordered Pate to jail for contempt of court, but the sentence was stayed pending Pate's appeal to the Court of Criminal Appeals, which later reversed Pate's conviction. Harris also subpoenaed Pate's tax records from the Oklahoma Tax Commission, which refused to release the documents unless ordered to do so by the Oklahoma Supreme Court.[19]

McCarty and Collins each appeared before the grand jury, each testifying for about three hours. Although their testimony remained secret, presumably both men denied any involvement in legislative bribery. Eventually, with their statutory time for a grand jury investigation expiring, the grand jury indicted only Pate for evading state income taxes, having decided that it did not have sufficient evidence to indict McCarty and Collins. The grand jury did issue a scathing report on the Oklahoma legislature, pointing out the existence of what they termed "money bills," a practice in which it was "not at all uncommon for funds to be gathered for the purpose of passing or killing legislation." They also found that "in many of our business community the payment of money to secure passage or defeat of legislation has come to be considered a normal business expense."[20] With the exception of Pate's tax charge, McCarty, Collins, and Pate had won. In the public eye, however, the credibility and legitimacy of state government had taken another serious blow.

Although the dog racing incident had resulted in no indictments of officeholders, the grand jury had exposed a serious defect in Oklahoma's government. The votes of certain members of the legislature, like those of some judges, appeared to be available to the highest bidder. This system had become such an integral part of the political fabric that many of those who wanted to accomplish anything requiring government approval took the influence- or vote-buying process for granted. In 1966 the voters would have the opportunity to demonstrate their displeasure with this situation.

Proposals for Reform

In May 1966, voters decided that 1966 would be the last year in Oklahoma history without a session of the legislature. In a state question placed on the runoff ballot, Oklahomans unexpectedly approved a constitutional amendment requiring the body to meet annually.[21] Reform forces took advantage of the absence of a legislature to prepare plans to change Oklahoma's judiciary.

The most ambitious of these was the Missouri plan, which became known in Oklahoma as the Sneed plan. The Missouri plan, enacted in 1940 in that state had enacted in as a response to the excesses of the Tom Pendergast machine, which controlled Missouri politics throughout the 1920s and 1930s, called for judicial vacancies to be filled by the governor from a list of three candidates submitted by a judicial nominating commission. The judge receiving the appointment would then be subject to a retention ballot to determine whether the judge remained on the bench. Judicial elections, partisan or nonpartisan, would be abolished, with the exception of the retention vote. The American Bar Association had supported judicial nominating commissions for years.

By 1966 several states had demonstrated considerable interest in some form of this mechanism. Kansas, reacting in part to a distasteful event in which the governor resigned in order to be appointed chief justice by the lieutenant governor, enacted a nominating commission in 1958. The next year Alaska was admitted to the union and constitutionally established its commission. Nebraska and Iowa enacted their versions in 1962. By 1967 Colorado, Vermont, Utah, and Idaho had followed suit. By 1977, nineteen states had established some form of the Missouri plan, although some of those states used judicial nomination committees only for appellate judgeships.[22]

Earl Sneed became the leading voice in Oklahoma for the adoption of the Missouri plan, and Oklahoma's proposal took his name. For fifteen years Sneed had been deeply interested in reforming Oklahoma's judiciary. A 1937 graduate of the University of Oklahoma (OU) School of Law, he had worked for the Tulsa Chamber of Commerce until World War II interrupted his career. After the war and with OU's law school expanding to accommodate returning service personnel, Acting Dean Maurice Merrill invited Sneed to teach at the school. In 1950 the thirty-seven-year-old Sneed was named the school's dean.[23]

The next year OU's law review published a study of Oklahoma's judicial system. The study found Oklahoma's system wanting, and it endorsed the Missouri plan, eventually adopted by Sneed. In 1954 Sneed asked his student Fred Harris, later a U.S. senator, to prepare a short synopsis of Oklahoma's confusing and overlapping court system. Harris came up with seven single-spaced pages just to describe Oklahoma's byzantine judicial framework. Of all of Oklahoma's judicial shortcomings, Sneed found the fee-based nature of the JP system the most outrageous; in Sneed's mind JP stood for "judgment for the plaintiff."[24]

Sneed began to look at entering electoral politics. He served from 1960 to 1964 as mayor of Norman and considered running for governor in 1962, eventually deciding against it. In October 1964 he told the press he would announce his plans by February of the next year, strongly indicating he would enter the 1966 gubernatorial race.[25] In September 1965 Sneed resigned from OU, taking a position with Liberty National Bank in Oklahoma City.[26] Although he opted not to run for governor, Sneed was a serious figure in Oklahoma's political and legal community.[27]

Rather than becoming a candidate himself, Sneed apparently decided to pursue his passion of reforming Oklahoma's judiciary. After the Supreme Court scandal broke, Governor Bellmon appointed a commission to study judicial reform. He named Sneed as the chair and also appointed Representative John McCune of Tulsa.[28] Sneed and McCune had very different ideas on the subject and would later clash over which path judicial reform should take.

At the insistence of Representative McCune, the legislative council had undertaken a comprehensive study of judicial reform, with an eye toward presenting a substantive and cohesive plan to the 1967 legislature. The council was originally composed of all fifty-two legislators; forty-nine of the legislators were also lawyers and three were nonlawyers. Some were more active than others, and eventually thirty legislators remained on the subcommittee through its conclusion.[29] The council took its job very seriously, holding numerous hearings and meetings and even traveling to Illinois, which utilized nonpartisan election, to study the judicial structure there.[30]

The Sneed forces, who had little legislative support and therefore needed to get their proposal before the people by initiative petition, struck first. On June 15, 1966, Sneed, Oklahoma Bar Association president Leroy Blackstock, and *Oklahoma City Times* editorial writer Clarke Thomas announced the formation of Judicial Reform Inc., an organization dedicated to the adoption of the Sneed plan. They stated they would file an initiative petition calling for a vote on their proposed constitutional amendment on August 26. The petition drive began with a sputtering and embarrassing start. On July 29 Blackstock, on behalf of Judicial Reform Inc., obtained official numbers from the secretary of state for an initiative petition and state question amending the state constitution with the Sneed plan, an action that proved to be a serious mistake.

Blackstock's intention had been merely to obtain numbers. However, under Oklahoma's initiative petition procedure, the act of receiving a number automatically began the ninety-day period for obtaining the 140,000 signatures necessary to put the petition on the ballot. The plan had been to organize, then file the petition on August 26, so Blackstock's error might have cost the reformers a month of organizational time, dooming the effort before it even began. Eventually, however, Secretary of State James Bullard allowed Judicial Reform to withdraw its petition, which the group refiled on August 23. Although the organization's competence came into temporary question, no permanent harm came to the petition drive.[31]

The Sneed plan proposed major changes to the judiciary. It called for four levels of courts: the Supreme Court, an intermediate-level appellate court, district courts, and appointed magistrates. The appellate judges and district judges would be selected by a judicial nominating commission, which would select three candidates. The governor would then appoint one of those three candidates to the position. With the exception of funding, the legislature would take little or no role in the judiciary. The chief justice would render decisions on personnel, assignments, and rulemaking. Justices of the peace would be abolished, as would the Court of Criminal Appeals. After six years, an appointed judge would be subject to a retention vote, in which the voter would answer the question, "Should Judge X be retained in office?"

The Sneed plan signature drive immediately ran into trouble. Despite enthusiastic participation by the League of Women Voters, by mid-October it became obvious the petition drive was stalling at substantially less than the required 140,000 signatures, a number which would later be considered too small by the plan's detractors. Over the next month, urban Oklahoma's newspapers, led by the *Daily Oklahoman* and *Oklahoma City Times,* launched editorial onslaughts urging voters to sign the petition. On October 19, in a front-page editorial titled "Have We Forgotten?," the editors reminded readers of the humiliation of the scandal and urged the adoption of the "well thought out" Sneed plan. Two days later, the paper quoted Clarke Thomas, its own editorial writer and secretary-treasurer of Judicial Reform as tying the plan to industrial growth, claiming Oklahoma's demonstrating that it had abolished "justice for sale" would help attract new industry to the state. The next week, in an editorial titled "We Need Best Judges," the paper heartily endorsed the Sneed plan, pointing out the need for taking judges out of politics. The writer, probably Thomas, argued that until 1846, judges were selected by appointment, not election, and therefore judicial appointment is the traditional American way. Dramatically, the author told readers that only two countries elect judges: "the United States and Communist Russia."[32] Other newspapers, including those from Tulsa, joined in the campaign for signatures.

One of the problems was the high number of signatures that Oklahoma's constitution required in order for a constitutional amendment to be placed on the ballot: 15 percent of the total votes cast in the last general election. One of the highest standards for initiative and referendum in the country, this criteria had been set by the overwhelmingly Democratic delegates of Oklahoma's 1907 constitutional convention. The 15 percent requirement drew no fire from Progressives at the time and passed the convention with little dissent.[33] This high number seems to have been a good-faith mistake by the drafters of the constitution, but it made things difficult for the Sneed plan proponents.

Even with the assistance of the metropolitan press, the Sneed plan signature campaign struggled. On November 4, with twelve days left before the deadline, Sneed said the petition had between forty thousand and fifty thousand signatures, far less than half the required number. Sneed announced a massive push to obtain the signatures. Judicial Reform, assisted by the League of Women Voters and parent-teacher association (PTA) groups, put seven thousand petitions in the hands of circulators, with eight thousand more to be supplied.[34]

Despite the distraction of the November 8 general election, the final days before the petition's deadline saw a tremendous increase of public interest in the petition promoting judicial reform. In the relatively small city of Chickasha, fourteen volunteers from the League of Women Voters obtained six hundred signatures in one day.[35] In Oklahoma City and Tulsa, members of the PTA conducted a door-to-door petition drive called "Light Up for Justice," which urged homeowners wishing to sign the petition to leave their porch lights on, so that a volunteer could easily identify a potential signer.[36] Eventually, the petitioner's backers presented the secretary of state's office with 142,377 signatures.[37]

Although backers of the Sneed plan did not know it then, it would be nearly two years until their judicial reform plan went to the voters for their consideration. Under Oklahoma's demanding procedure for initiative petitions, backers of a petition were required to obtain 15 percent of the "last" general election votes. Once the petition was turned in, Oklahoma secretary of state John Rogers had the duty to verify the signatures and to determine if the requirement had been satisfied. The Sneed plan petition had begun before the 1966 election but had been turned in after the election had occurred. The 1966 election drew a considerably smaller turnout than the election of 1964, which had featured a presidential election as well as the hotly contested U.S. Senate contest between Fred R. Harris and Bud Wilkinson. If the "last" general election meant 1964's election, the petition drive had fallen twenty-three votes short of the mark. If "last" were interpreted as the election of 1966, the petition would go to the voters.[38]

Rogers obtained an opinion from Attorney General Charles Nesbitt, who advised him to follow the numbers from the 1966 election. On April 25, Rogers approved the petition; opponents immediately appealed the decision, which put the election on hold pending an appellate ruling. In the meantime, 1967 was an off-year for elections, and Governor Bartlett did not call for a special election. The Sneed plan would not go before the voters until 1968, nearly two years after the petitions being turned in to the secretary of state.

The legislature took advantage of the time between sessions to study and debate judicial reform. The strong consensus of the legislative reformers was to achieve court reform but retain judicial elections. Prior to the 1966 election, the legislative subcommittee came up with the bare bones of a plan to be presented to the entire legislature in January. By August the council had agreed on a proposed reorganization of the trial courts. Under the legislative proposal, the posts of county judge, juvenile judge, and justice of the peace were to be abolished. The position of associate district judge would be created as an elective post, guaranteeing one judge for each of the seventy-seven counties. The associate district judge would have general jurisdiction with the authority to hear any type of case. The plan also included the creation of the post of special district judge, who would be appointed by the district judges, to handle smaller civil cases, misdemeanors, and preliminary felony matters. Courts of common pleas and special sessions would also be abolished. In an issue of enormous importance to the legislature, control of creation of courts, allocation of judicial resources, and the number of judges would be decided by the legislature, not the chief justice, as in the Sneed plan. The committee rejected the concept of putting near-total control of the courts in the hands of the chief justice.[39]

In September the subcommittee revealed its proposal for reforming the appellate courts. Although most states did not have appeals courts exclusively for criminal cases, the legislative proposal retained the Court of Criminal

Appeals, which would have been abolished under the Sneed plan. It also created intermediate civil courts of appeal and the office of court administrator, as well as directing that the office of clerk of the Supreme Court be an appointed, rather than an elected, position.[40]

At the suggestion of Senator Anthony Massad of Frederick, the committee decided to submit the proposal to the voters in two separate questions: one on streamlining the court system and the other on judicial selection. Massad thought court reorganization would pass easily, unless it were tied to judicial selection. The two questions would therefore be submitted separately to help ensure the passage of the court reorganization plan. On October 28, only eleven days before the general election, the committee submitted its plan for judicial selection, which called for nonpartisan election of judges at the appellate and trial levels; the only exception would be the newly created special district judges, who would be appointed by trial judges. Two senators, Massad and Roy Grantham, dissented; each preferred some version of a system in which appellate judges were appointed and trial judges elected.[41]

Oklahoma now had two competing court reform proposals on the table, either of which would constitute a vast improvement over the existing structure. Both plans fixed the state's confusing and contradictory jurisdictional issues by establishing one district court. Both abolished partisan judicial elections and the justice of the peace system. Each called for administration of the courts by a court administrator. Only the legislative plan called for a separate Court of Criminal Appeals, while only the Sneed plan authorized the continuation of municipal courts.

There were other substantial differences, one that involved how judges would be selected. The cornerstone of the Sneed plan was judicial selection; all judges would be appointed, with all judges except magistrates being screened by the judicial nominating commission, then selected by the governor. The legislative plan called for all but special district judges to be elected on a nonpartisan ballot.

One difference was irreconcilable. The Sneed plan gave entire authority for creation of judgeships, creation of judicial districts, and assignment of personnel to the chief justice, with the legislature only being involved in the appropriation of money. The legislature's plan specifically reserved those tasks to itself. Oklahoma's legislature would never have voluntarily surrendered those rights.

Under the legislative plan, the Oklahoma constitution would provide for the office of one associate district judge for every county, regardless of the county's population. The concept of not having at least one judge per county was anathema to rural voters, who were already apprehensive about their diminishing role in state politics. The Sneed plan, which provided for judicial assignments from Oklahoma City, had little to offer rural voters.

Debating the merits of the two plans obscured another question about court reform. Oklahoma law required any change to its constitution to be approved by the electorate. No one knew whether conservative Oklahoma voters would support any sort of serious change to their legal structure. The respective merits of the Sneed plan and the legislature's plan were moot if voters saw no need to change the system.

The 1966 Campaign

Republican Henry Bellmon's gubernatorial victory in 1962 was widely seen as an aberration, and the 1966 governor's race drew intense interest, especially from Democrats. Thirteen Democrats, including former governor Raymond Gary, Attorney General Charles Nesbitt, Oklahoma City attorney Preston Moore, Tulsa district attorney David Hall, State Senator Cleeta John Rogers, and Oklahoma City publisher J. Leland Gourley filed for the party's nomination. Three Republicans filed. Only two of the three, Tulsa state senator Dewey F. Bartlett and Waukomis banker John N. (Happy) Camp were serious candidates.[42]

We now know that 1966 was a year of enormous progress for the Republican Party, both in the South and nationally, showing the party's recovery from the 1964 debacle. Signaling the change was the reemergence of Richard Nixon and the unexpected landslide election of former actor Ronald Reagan as governor of California. In the South, U.S. senator John Tower of Texas, whose surprise 1961 victory had been seen as a fluke, was reelected, and Howard Baker of Tennessee defeated a former governor for a seat in the U.S. Senate. The political scene in Oklahoma conformed with these national trends.

The Oklahoma judiciary and bar received yet another black eye when Judge Kirksey Nix, who was serving on the Court of Criminal Appeals, filed for the Democratic nomination as attorney general. Nix refused to give up his seat on the Court of Criminal Appeals, completely ignoring an Oklahoma statute that clearly required a judge running for a nonjudicial office to resign. The Oklahoma Bar Association, at the instance of OBA president and judicial reformer Leroy Blackstock, took Nix to the Supreme Court, which then referred the matter back to the OBA.[43] Nix lamely explained his refusal to resign by explaining that Governor Bellmon would fill a vacancy on the Court of Criminal Appeals with a Republican, thus increasing the public perception of a judicial seat as a political office. Judge Nix remained on the ballot; he came in second in the Democratic primary, then withdrew before the runoff.[44]

Most of the gubernatorial candidates favored some version of court reform. Of the Democrats, Nesbitt and Rogers favored the Sneed plan. Several other Democrats, including Gary, supported appointment of appellate judges and nonpartisan election of trial judges. Moore opposed an appointive system and favored continued election of all judges. On the Republican side, Bartlett favored the Sneed plan, while Camp supported continued election of judges.[45]

In the May 3 primary, Raymond Gary took a substantial lead, which eventually grew to fifty-six thousand votes. Oklahoma City attorney Preston Moore narrowly made the runoff against Gary, edging out Tulsa prosecutor David Hall. Bartlett narrowly led Camp in the voting for the Republican nomination, but the race was so close that the few votes for a third candidate forced Oklahoma's first Republican gubernatorial runoff.[46]

Voters in the May 3 primary election also approved State Question 431, which established a court on the Judiciary, finally providing a practical vehicle to remove corrupt, incompetent, or infirm judges from office. State Question 431 had met with little or no opposition, and it passed easily. The formidable and time-consuming task of removing judges by impeachment would not happen again. Oklahoma voters also approved a constitutional amendment allowing governors to serve two terms, ending the requirement that a governor leave office after four years.[47]

In the three weeks between the primary election and the runoff, Gary's rurally based campaign lost steam. Moore, helped by low pro-Gary rural turnout, easily overcame his fifty-six-thousand vote deficit in the primary and defeated Gary by about thirty thousand votes. Thanks in part to a huge majority in Tulsa County, Bartlett defeated Camp for the Republican nomination.[48]

Although he was a lawyer, Preston Moore's real interests were politics and the American Legion. A veteran of the World War II Pacific theatre, Moore became the legion's state commander while he was still in law school. His legion work allowed him access to national politics, and in 1960 he directed Lyndon Johnson's presidential campaign in Oklahoma. Two years later he ran for governor, finishing third to Bill Atkinson and Raymond Gary. Moore endorsed Atkinson in the runoff, a decision that embittered Gary. This fact would become significant four years later.[49]

Dewey Bartlett represented an Oklahoma that was becoming more urban and urbane. Bartlett had grown up in Ohio, graduated from Princeton University, then served in the Marine Corps during World War II. After the war, Bartlett moved to Tulsa, joining his father's oil company. He successfully ran for the State Senate in 1962. He would become the first Roman Catholic to become governor of Oklahoma. Unusually for a politician, Bartlett was a publicly solemn, shy man with little desire for small talk.[50]

Moore entered the general election campaign with a huge lead, and it became obvious that his strategy was, in the words of an *Oklahoma City Times* reporter, "Don't rock the boat."[51] An aggressive Republican campaign became a serious problem for Moore. His legal practice had concentrated on labor-management arbitration, prompting Republicans to run ads cryptically asking, "What does Preston Moore really do for a living?"[52] Moore became his own worst enemy, as he repeatedly evaded being pinned down on issues, allowing Bartlett to portray him as indecisive and equivocating. As the *Tulsa World* put it, "Republicans say they are attacking Preston Moore on all the firm stands he took before he wised up and changed them."[53]

This was true of court reform. Moore clearly established himself as an advocate of judicial elections and an opponent of the Missouri plan; other than that, it was hard to discern his position. Moore vaguely said he was for "modernization and streamlining of the courts," but he never explained exactly what he had in mind. He took the vague, indecisive, and evasive step of appointing his own committee to study court reform, thus kicking the issue under the table.[54]

In early October, Moore sent his Oklahoma County campaign chairman to a meeting of justices of the peace, a meeting whose purpose was to defeat the Sneed plan. He also tried to persuade the legislative committee to back away from the idea of abolishing JPs and wrote the JP organization a letter indicating that he would use his power as governor to retain them. Moore's only specific proposed reform was the abolition of JP's fee-based compensation system.[55] On the whole, although Moore said he was for court reform, his actions revealed otherwise.

Bartlett strongly endorsed the concept of appointing appellate judges. He impractically suggested that "local units" could decide on the appropriate system for selecting trial judges.[56] This led *Oklahoman* columnist Ray Parr to comment that Bartlett was "neither for nor against the Sneed plan," while Moore was "all for judicial reform as long as we don't change anything."⁵⁷

As the campaign progressed, Moore lost ground to Bartlett. Gary, avenging Moore's endorsement of his opponent four years earlier, declined to endorse Moore, stating simply that he and Moore didn't "see eye to eye on governmental problems."⁵⁸ The *Daily Oklahoman* and *Oklahoma City Times* ran strong editorials opposing Moore, calling him a "political backslapper" and an "arranger."⁵⁹ Bartlett also exploited the declining popularity of the Democratic Party, asking voters, "If my opponent is elected governor, who will really be the governor—LBJ or J. D. McCarty?"⁶⁰

In the meantime, McCarty was having his own problems with his reelection campaign. A Republican, Vondel Smith, had entered the race for McCarty's seat in the legislature. Reapportionment had changed McCarty's district; instead of being largely confined to Capitol Hill in southwest Oklahoma City, it now included parts of Midwest City and Del City, fast-growing municipalities that had barely existed when McCarty entered the legislature. These cities close to Tinker Air Force Base contained newer voters and homes.⁶¹ Eager to get rid of McCarty, Republican activists drew up lists of every family, where they worked, what church they attended, how many children they had, and other pertinent information. By the week before the election, Smith claimed to have contacted everyone in the district, and Republicans were very optimistic about their chances of ousting McCarty from the legislature. In their advertising, Republicans said nothing about McCarty's problems with the grand jury and the racing interests, simply running Smith's photograph, name, and the legislative district he sought to represent.⁶²

Always the astute political strategist, McCarty realized that he was in trouble and expressed his worry to his political allies.⁶³ No friend of Oklahoma City's daily newspapers, he nevertheless advertised heavily in them, describing his political and philanthropic accomplishments and telling readers, "When there's work to be done . . . J.D. McCarty is Oklahoma's Man of Action." The Saturday before the election, McCarty ran a full-page ad in the *Oklahoma City Times*, citing his awards for contributions to mental health and cerebral palsy.⁶⁴ McCarty told audiences, "Those boys in their ivory tower at Fourth and Broadway [the *Oklahoman* and *Times*] have stayed up nights trying to do two things—slanting the news columns and writing editorials to take away the power of Oklahomans to elect their judges, and trying to destroy Preston J. Moore."⁶⁵

Election Day featured good weather, and voter turnout was heavy. The 1966 Oklahoma election resulted in overwhelming victories for Republicans and a debacle for Democrats, making the result the best for the Oklahoma GOP since 1928.[66] Bartlett, aided by huge majorities in Oklahoma and Tulsa Counties, easily defeated Moore by a final total of 377,078 to 296,328. In Tulsa County, Bartlett beat Moore by more than a two-to-one margin. G. T. Blankenship, who had exposed the court scandal on the House floor, became the first Republican attorney general in Oklahoma history. Blankenship campaigned on a slogan of "He uncovered the court scandals," publishing a cartoon of Blankenship pointing his finger of three fleeing judges in robes. Republicans also elected the state labor commissioner, making three statewide victories for the party.[67]

U.S. senator Fred Harris, who had expected a huge victory against token Republican opposition, struggled but was reelected, although by a much closer margin than he had expected. Over the next six years, Harris would move sharply to the left, even in relation to the national party and certainly far away from his conservative constituents in Oklahoma. He found himself unable and unwilling to stand for reelection in 1972, opting for a short-lived and quixotic campaign for the Democratic presidential nomination. In southwestern Oklahoma, Republican James V. Smith unseated Democratic congressman Jed Johnson. Republicans also picked up seven seats in the legislature.

One of those seven legislative seats changing parties was McCarty's. After McCarty's thirteen terms in the legislature, Vondel Smith defeated the Speaker by almost a two-to-one margin, ending McCarty's political career. In 1967 McCarty was indicted and convicted on federal charges of income tax evasion. The charges on which he was found guilty involved undeclared income from various entities, including the Oklahoma City Chamber of Commerce, paying McCarty in exchange for political favors. He was acquitted of charges involving the horse racing and dog racing bills. After his release from prison, he continued to be involved with politics but never held public office again.

McCarty had indeed been an ironfisted speaker with a fearsome temper and a fierce resistance to change, but he had also done some very good things. With his encyclopedic knowledge of state government and state politics, McCarty knew how to get things done. He had been a good friend to Oklahoma's schools and colleges and had demonstrated enormous empathy for Oklahoma's mentally ill, mentally challenged children, and children suffering from cerebral palsy.[68] After McCarty's 1981 death the Oklahoma legislature renamed the Norman center for children with developmental disabilities the J. D. McCarty Center.

It is tempting to speculate on what might have happened to court reform if McCarty had remained Speaker. McCarty had declared his implacable hostility to Sneed's plan for appointed judges and his unwavering support for judicial elections. On the other hand, with McCarty as Speaker, the legislative council had publicly studied and debated the issue for two years. While McCarty had not publicly participated in the council, there is no evidence that he interfered with their work or tried to stop the meetings. Had McCarty intended to kill court reform outright, he had no reason to allow the legislature to give the issue momentum. He also had the referendum on the Sneed plan, which he hated, hanging over his head, pending the outcome of litigation. McCarty would have wanted to deflect Sneed's plan. Had he remained in office, McCarty likely would have allowed some sort of court reform—probably nonpartisan election of all judges—to be submitted to the people.

Had Preston Moore been elected governor, his embrace of the justices of the peace would have made court reform a near impossibility. Abolition of the JP office, with its inherent amateurism and conflicts of interest, was the cornerstone of any meaningful improvement in Oklahoma's judicial system. Substantial change in the judiciary would have required enactment without the governor's support.

The results in Oklahoma were consistent with the nationwide trend. Two years after his landslide victory, President Johnson's political support declined precipitously. Americans recoiled from huge increases in public spending, the expansion of the federal government, the passage of civil rights legislation, the expansion of the Vietnam War, and enactment of social welfare legislation. The rise of the Republican Party in the South had begun. Nationally, California elected as governor Ronald Reagan, who quickly became an icon for conservative Republicans. The campaign also brought renewed legitimacy to the political fortunes of Richard Nixon, who campaigned tirelessly and effectively for Republican candidates across the country, acquiring political capital for his presidential race two years later.

In Oklahoma the 1966 election validated the Republican Party and proved that Bellmon's 1962 victory was not a fluke. For three gubernatorial elections in a row, Oklahomans had selected a reform-minded candidate to lead the state and rejected the conservative, antireform establishment. Oklahoma Republicans had capitalized on public satisfaction with Governor Bellmon's term and offered a better and larger slate of candidates than it had previously offered.[69] With their votes in 1966, Oklahoma's electorate demonstrated weariness with business as usual and the desire for honesty and integrity in the state capitol.

The election of Bartlett and the defeat of McCarty helped create a political climate friendly to court reform. If either election had gone differently, any change in Oklahoma's judiciary would have taken a different course. The looming referendum on the Sneed plan weighed heavily on the Oklahoma legislature as it prepared for its 1967 session. If the legislature were to create a court system that met its own criteria, the time was at hand.

❖ 6
Enactment of Legislative Reform and Defeat of the Sneed Plan

The Oklahoma electorate had signaled its desire to change from the rural conservative politics of the state's first decades. With the elections of Edmondson, Bellmon, and Bartlett, Oklahomans had selected governors three times in succession who had no ties to the legislative establishment. McCarty's defeat, coming amid the allegations of scandal, also indicated that voters were fed up with their state government. The growing public disillusionment with the state's politics should not be seen in terms of liberal versus conservative. Oklahomans in the 1960s remained solidly conservative in their politics and, by their votes in 1966, had resoundingly rejected the big-government policies of Lyndon Johnson. Instead, the changing trend represented two themes: the state's shifting demographics and voter resentment at being excluded from governmental decision making by special interests meeting behind closed doors.

McCarty's defeat meant the position of Speaker of the House had unexpectedly opened. Rex Privett of Maramac immediately became a candidate. Although Representative Jerry Sokolosky of Oklahoma City claimed to have obtained the support of younger, urban legislators for a different candidate, Privett moved quickly and clinched the position, securing the votes of sixty-nine out of a possible seventy-four Democratic representatives. In his acceptance speech, Privett turned the page, saying, "I do not condemn the past speaker, but I realize that the past is gone and the future is ahead. It is our duty to change the image of the legislature."

Privett quickly established his control of the House of Representatives, keeping some of McCarty's team but not consulting with McCarty.[1] Promising a greater role for urban legislators, Privett outlined five problems the legislature needed to address: education, court reform, congressional redistricting, penal reform, and improvement in mental institutions. On the subject of court reform, Privett expressed his preference for nonpartisan election of all judges and the submission of proposed state questions on one ballot, not the two ballots proposed by the legislative committee.[2]

Dewey Bartlett was inaugurated as governor on January 10, 1967. In his inaugural address, Bartlett stated, "I have prepared for introduction a constitutional amendment for the selection of appellate judges by appointment, rather than election." Bartlett demonstrated his seriousness on the subject of a judicial nominating commission by announcing his own voluntary judicial nominating commission to make recommendations on vacancies occurring during his term. Bartlett's voluntary plan called for a commission consisting of six attorneys elected by the Oklahoma Bar Association and seven laypeople, four from one party and three from the other, to nominate three candidates for judicial openings. Bartlett would then select one of those three candidates for the position.[3]

As the parties negotiated judicial reform, the state government and the legal community faced yet another embarrassing and troubling scandal involving attorneys and undue influence. This one involved the Corporation Commission, a regulatory agency composed of three commissioners elected in statewide elections, which governs, among other things, utility rates and portions of the oil and gas industry. In March and April 1967 the legislature and public learned that the late Clyde Hale Sr., who had been an attorney and lobbyist for Oklahoma Natural Gas (ONG), had regularly paid fees to James Welch and William L. Anderson, full-time attorneys for the commission, while the utility had rate-increase cases pending before the commission. Welch, during the time he was chief counsel for the Corporation Commission, received more than $12,500 from Hale. In one instance Welch, who was making $10,000 per year as a salaried attorney for the commission, received a fee of $5,375 from ONG shortly after he wrote an order approving ONG's request for a $4.3-million-per-year rate increase.[4]

Hale's son, Clyde Jr., also claimed that ONG had, through his father, made significant cash contributions to the campaigns of commissioners Roy Jones and Harold Freeman, a practice that violated Oklahoma's law barring corporations from giving political donations. The commissioners had also allegedly accepted lavish entertainment from ONG, including annual trips to the Oklahoma-Texas football game and trips to the horse track at Hot Springs, Arkansas. Attorneys practicing before the commission routinely made cash contributions toward political campaigns, a practice that Freeman explained by arguing, "If they all kick in, that must mean we are doing a good job."

Freeman and Jones had also purchased shares in a Pauls Valley oilfield supply company. Freeman then solicited and received business for the company from ONG and Sunray DX, both regulated by the Corporation Commission.[5]

A legislative committee headed by Senator Roy Grantham investigating the commission's affairs eventually found the witnesses, including lawyers Welch and Hale Jr., so unworthy of belief that the committee was unable to determine with precision exactly what had happened. The panel also found that Hale Jr., Welch, Anderson, and a fourth attorney had violated legal ethics and referred the matter to the Oklahoma Bar Association.[6] The scandal gradually drifted out of public attention, but the bar and the state government suffered another black eye.

Since the legislature now met annually, legislators had a personal financial incentive to minimize the session's length. As one legislator put it, "I used to have eighteen months to go home and make some money. With annual sessions, we'll have to keep them short or we'll have to get out." Senate president pro tempore Clem McSpadden announced a goal of adjournment by May 1, which would mean the session would last less than four months.[7]

By the end of March, judicial reform had stalled in the State Senate. The House of Representatives passed a bill abolishing JPs and placing all judges on a nonpartisan ballot. The Senate was expected to call for the appointment of appellate judges. Political prognosticators expected the process to take a few weeks.[8]

Both houses of the legislature were able to agree on some concepts, while others were more controversial. Both agreed on reorganization of the courts, with the creation of district judges, associate district judges, and special judges. The houses agreed that each county would be guaranteed an associate district judge. The Court of Criminal Appeals, a court that did not exist in most states, would continue operations. Oklahoma's common pleas courts, superior courts, and other specialized courts were to be abolished.

The two houses were unable to agree on the process for the selection of appellate judges. The idea of a judicial nominating commission held little appeal in the House of Representatives, which overwhelmingly favored direct election of all judges on a nonpartisan ballot. The concept of a commission had considerably more support in the Senate, but even in that chamber, appellate judge appointment met with serious opposition.[9]

By late April the idea of appointive appellate judges was in such trouble that the entire issue of court reform was threatened. The House passed a package authorizing a vote on reforming the courts with all judges elected on a nonpartisan basis. Although McSpadden, the Senate's leader, favored appellate judge appointment, the Senate voted in favor of all judges being elected. Speaker Privett was opposed to the idea of the judicial nomination commission, and he declared that he had no reason to believe the House would ever vote in favor of it. Surprisingly, Bartlett, the leading proponent of the judicial nominating commission concept, went more than three months without discussing the proposal with Privett.[10]

The parties began to make progress when Bartlett, McSpadden, and Privett spoke about the subject over breakfast on April 24. The constant threat of the Sneed plan made essential the formation of a legislative plan acceptable to the voters, thus providing motivation to reach a solution. The Sneed plan vote became even more problematic for legislators the next day, when Secretary of State John Rogers finally upheld the validity of the signatures on the Sneed plan initiative petition, leaving an appeal to the Oklahoma Supreme Court as the final barrier to the plan being submitted to the voters. Court reform was also the last remaining issue in the legislative session, so the desire to go home also added a sense of urgency.[11]

Although the breakfast by no means settled the dispute, the leaders generally agreed to submit both issues—appellate appointment and nonpartisan election of all judges—to the voters and allow the electorate to decide which proposal, if either, it wanted.[12] The legislature's primary opposition to a judicial nominating commission was the governor's power to appoint six of its thirteen members. Some legislators were reluctant to cede so much power to the governor, leading Senator Robert Gee to suggest that the governor appoint two members, with the other four to be named by the Speaker of the House and the president pro tempore of the Senate.

On Sunday, May 7, the conference committees reached an agreement on most of the legislation. Bartlett's insistence on a judicial nominating commission overcame the legislature's general distaste for the concept, and the commission remained in the proposal. Privett's insistence on a quick election resulted in a special election date of July 11, only two months away. Bartlett agreed to a nonpartisan election of trial judges and the three-tiered system consisting of district judges, associate district judges, and special judges at the trial level; a civil court of appeals; and a court of criminal appeals. The Supreme Court would have the final word on civil appeals and court supervision. The office of court administrator, which would administer budgets and personnel from Oklahoma City, would also be created. For the moment, the question of who would be responsible for naming the members of the nominating committee remained unresolved.[13]

A final agreement on the proposal came the next day from the conference committee and the governor. Court reform would be submitted to the people on colored ballots. Court reorganization would appear on a white ballot, while the judicial nominating commission ballot would be yellow. If court reorganization failed, the judicial nominating commission would automatically fail as well. The nominating commission would comprise thirteen members, six of whom would be elected from the Oklahoma Bar Association and another six appointed by the governor. The thirteenth commissioner would be appointed by the other twelve members. Three days later the legislature adopted the proposal, authorized the July election, and adjourned.[14]

The passage of the proposed constitutional amendments reflected very well on the legislative process. If the plan were approved by the voters, the legislature had abolished the antiquated and ethically suspect justice of the peace system. They had modernized and centralized the court structure, as well as taking a strong step toward professionalizing the judiciary. Despite the differences in political parties, the legislature and the governor had successfully compromised and reached a workable proposal. Bartlett had his nominating commission, if only for appellate judges and midterm trial court vacancies, while the House had been able to limit the use of the commission to those instances. Representative John McCune told his fellow committee members, "This is a better way to beat the Missouri plan. . . . If both resolutions pass, appointment of judges will stop at the appellate level."[15]

The 1967 Special Election

One of the legislation's problems was its complexity. With the broad nature of the proposal and the contingent nature of the yellow and white ballots, the danger of confusing and boring the electorate was very real. For the huge majority of Oklahomans not normally involved in the details of politics and law, the proposal was puzzling; only a motivated voter would take the time to analyze the issues in detail. The complicated nature of the proposals would prove to be problematic on July 11.

Voters had less than two months in which to consider State Questions 447 and 448. This proved to be plenty of time for reform advocates. The only really organized opposition to the questions came from the Oklahoma American

Federation of Labor–Congress of Industrial Organizations (AFL-CIO), which endorsed the idea of nonpartisan elections but strongly opposed the concept of the judicial nominating commission. Jack Odom, the executive vice president of the organization, said he did not "trust the Republican administration" to name nonpartisan judges. The state organization of the Oklahoma Democratic Party listened to Odom's request for assistance but took no action on SQ 447 and 448.[16] The Oklahoma League of Women Voters, leading backers of the Sneed plan, considered the legislative plan an improvement over the existing system, endorsing the state questions while maintaining their strong preference for the Sneed plan.[17]

In the days after the legislature's adjournment, the proponents debated what to do. Bartlett had pushed for court reform, and he was seen as laying his prestige on the line for the issue. The Oklahoma Republican Party favored the reform, but its leaders were unsure—given their status as a minority party—about whether to campaign publicly for the questions. The Oklahoma Democratic Party was also unsure of what course to take. The Democrats were trying to shed their image of portraying, as Otis Sullivant put it, "an old guard, rural-dominated opposition to progress" but had no wish to enhance Bartlett's standing with the voters.[18]

As the date for the election drew closer, the parties began to back away from the issue of court reform. The campaign, such as it was, fell between the cracks. State Question 448, which reorganized the courts and made judicial elections nonpartisan, met virtually no organized opposition. The only real exception came from some county officials, who feared a loss of revenue generated by the JP courts. The legislative council quickly agreed to support legislation guaranteeing that counties would not lose revenue, and the public objections faded away.[19]

State Question 447, the proposal for the judicial nominating commission for appellate judges and filling openings on the trial bench, drew considerably more fire than SQ 448. Senator John Young of Sapulpa, a vociferous opponent of the commission, wrote, "The vested interests in the name of reform are trying to sell the people on the yellow ballot, wherein they would be deprived of their right to elect judges. . . . The judicial reformers are telling the people that the lawyers of the Oklahoma Bar Association and heavy campaign supporters of the governor, who are named on the commission, are better citizens than the rest of us and should have the exclusive right of selecting the people's judges."[20]

For the most part, though, the campaign was very quiet. With the exception of one sparsely attended public meeting at the Oklahoma Bar Center, Bartlett, who had the most to lose if the state questions failed, remained out of the fray. On July 5, six days before the election, Bartlett spoke at a civic luncheon in Duncan, which was celebrating its seventy-fifth anniversary as a city. His remarks centered on persuading his audience to "sell Oklahoma"; the newspaper account of his speech did not mention the pending court reform election.[21] Bartlett's absence from the nonexistent campaign was also noted by *Oklahoman* columnist Ray Parr, who noted in his folksy manner, "I got to admire Governor Bartlett's technique in this campaign. He is for 'em just enough so he can claim credit if they are adopted but is not out in front far enough that folks can claim he suffered a political defeat in case they lose."[22]

Why Bartlett did not take a more active role in the campaign is unclear. Although his papers are silent on the subject, it is obvious from the context that Governor Bartlett was quite cognizant of his status as a Republican governor in a Democratic state. Bartlett likely thought that his taking the lead would make the issue more partisan—and its defeat more likely.

The state's press saw its role primarily as educating the public on the nature of the issues. Most newspapers printed articles explaining the state questions and the respective meanings of the yellow and white ballots. Only in the few days just before the election did the issue receive editorial coverage. The *Oklahoman* and the *Duncan Banner* urged their readers to vote in favor of the issue while the southeastern Oklahoma *Durant Daily Democrat*, citing the complicated nature of the proposals, recommended against it. In rural Grant County in northern Oklahoma, at the local legislator's suggestion the *Medford Patriot-Star* published a long story explaining the questions. The author ended the article by commenting, "In summary, if you want court reorganization but wish to ELECT judges, vote yes on 448 and no on 447."[23]

Most of the news coverage revolved around the lack of public interest in the special election. The *Duncan Banner* reported, "Spot polls have indicated a majority of citizens do not even know there is a statewide election, let alone what will be on the ballot."[24] In his column Ray Parr expressed skepticism about the entire measure. Referring to the lack of public interest, he wrote, "You suppose there is any chance of this judicial reform election ending in a scoreless tie? Wonder whatever happened to all the indignation over our present system a while back?" He added, "Not many legislators are going out on a limb for the amendments, on account they weren't very enthusiastic about 'em in the first place when they submitted 'em. It was just something to get people's mind off the Sneed plan." Finally, Parr expressed doubt about the wisdom of submitting constitutional amendments at a special election, when "such a small minority can change or refuse to change Oklahoma's fundamental law."[25]

The frustrated Parr had overstated his case. Legislators like McCune, Gee, and Anthony Massad worked countless hours on the state questions and had given the subject enormous study and thought. Although the questions were unquestionably designed as an alternative to the Sneed plan, the legislators and governor had a lot of which to be proud. However, it was true that the plan, achieved through compromise, had no real author, thus no real champion to plead the merits of the proposal to the public.

In the last few days before the election, a small number of political advertisements opposing the state questions appeared in some newspapers. An unsigned ad, which appeared in the *Marietta Monitor* in southern Oklahoma and several other newspapers, argued, "If you are capable of electing your Governor, you are certainly capable of electing your judges. . . . Do you want more taxes? Would you like to support a system of courts that in all probability you will never use? . . . The so-called Judicial Reform plan will cost the taxpayers of Oklahoma $1,450,000 per year."[26] The day before the election, sixty Oklahoma County lawyers signed an advertisement opposing the state questions. The attorneys objected both to the abolition of the justice of the peace courts and the appointment of judges.[27]

Predictions of a light turnout on July 11 proved correct. Only about 165,000 Oklahomans voted in the special election. Aided by huge majorities in the Oklahoma City and Tulsa area, both state questions passed. State Question 448 was approved with 55 percent of the vote, while State Question 447, the judicial nominating commission, received 52 percent approval.

Two facts stand out from the election results. First, the vote margin in favor of court reorganization, State Question 448, was surprisingly slim. The legislature and the governor had stacked the deck in favor of the measure, setting it for a quick special election in which the courts were the only issue on the ballot and providing a separate, contingent ballot for the judicial nominating commission. The campaign against SQ 448 was minimal. Nevertheless, with these advantages, only 55 percent of the voters, all of whom had made a special trip to the polls just to cast a ballot on the questions, voted for it.

Second, the special election of July 11 illustrates the enormous fissure between the urban and rural areas of Oklahoma. In Oklahoma County, out of nearly 29,000 votes cast, State Question 447 received 74 percent of the vote, while voters there approved SQ 448 by 78 percent. Tulsa County's members were similar. Out of approximately 27,000 votes cast, about 75 percent of the voters approved SQ 447 and 78 percent approved SQ 448. SQ 448, the court reorganization question, carried only eleven counties: Canadian, Cleveland, Garfield, Muskogee, Oklahoma, Ottawa, Payne, Pontotoc, Stephens, Tulsa, and Washington. SQ 447, the judicial appointment measure, passed only nine counties, as Canadian and Pontotoc Counties narrowly voted it down. Out of seventy-seven counties, SQ 447 failed in sixty-eight of them, while SQ 448 failed in sixty-six.

Some of the vote totals are noteworthy. In staunchly Democratic Love County in southern Oklahoma, 62 people voted in favor of SQ 448, and 642 against it; only 9 percent of Love County voters approved of court reorganization. In Grant County, a northern Oklahoma county that tended to support Republicans, 370 people voted in favor of SQ 448 and 945 against. In neither case did the local newspaper take an editorial position. Both measures failed in well-populated counties like Comanche, Creek, Kay, LeFlore, Pottawatomie, and Sequoyah.

Proponents of the state questions simply had not made a convincing case for change to conservative rural Oklahomans. The questions were complex and far-reaching; SQ 447, which had the lower number, was contingent on the passage of SQ 448. No one had led an effective statewide campaign in favor of the questions, and Governor Bartlett had, for the most part, remained quiet on the issue in the month before the election. The guarantee of an associate district judge was not enough to persuade rural Oklahomans that the state questions benefited them.

Moreover, the period of the 1960s was a time of great concern for rural Oklahomans. While the population of the state had increased only slightly, from 2,233,351 to 2,328,284 during the period from 1950 to 1960, the demographics had changed enormously. Seeing opportunity in the cities, Oklahomans were moving to urban areas in enormous numbers. Between 1950 and 1960 Oklahoma City grew 33.2 percent, from a population of 243,504 to 324,253; Tulsa's population grew from 182,740 to 261,685, an increase of 43.2 percent. The Oklahoma City suburbs of Midwest City, Del City, and The Village, which did not exist until after World War II, now housed 36,058, 12,934, and 12,118 people, respectively. Smaller cities grew exponentially as well; Lawton grew 77.3 percent, from 34,737 to 61,697 people, while the population of Altus increased from 9,735 to 20,184, an increase of 118 percent. Bartlesville's population increased 45.1 percent.

Rural counties saw declines in their population, some of which were precipitous. Cotton County, in southwest Oklahoma, saw a 30 percent decrease in its population between 1950 and 1960. Grant County, located on the Kansas border, lost 22.2 percent of its population, while McIntosh County, in the eastern part of the state, saw a 30.6 percent decline. Overall, rural Oklahoma's population declined 21.1 percent during the 1950s, while urban Oklahoma's population increased 28.6 percent.[28]

The same trend continued throughout the 1960s. Communities of fewer than ten thousand saw their population decline about 10 percent, while cities of more than ten thousand saw a proportionate increase. Tulsa's population increased 26 percent, while the Tulsa suburb of Sand Springs grew 48 percent in the 1960s.

Rural Oklahomans, therefore, found themselves in crisis. The state's urbanization meant that rural Oklahomans were losing businesses and access to health care. If they chose to sell their home, few buyers were in the market to purchase them. In small communities, abandoning the JP system also had little appeal. The JP system, however flawed, was cheap and business-friendly. In a small-town environment, a vote to abolish JPs was also a vote to put a neighbor and acquaintance out of a job. Although the legislative plan guaranteed at least one judge per county, rural counties already had that with the county judge system. The centralization of judicial authority in Oklahoma City constituted another nail, however small, in the coffin of rural Oklahoma.

The 1968 Legislature

Despite rural opposition, the state questions had passed, and the legislative reform had become part of Oklahoma's constitution. It now became the duty of the 1968 legislature to enact the necessary statutes and make the appropriations to implement the reform. While the 1967 session had featured bipartisanship, the 1968 version quickly became rancorous.

Public education, which had largely been ignored the previous year, became the focal point of the legislature's 1968 business. Even as the 1967 session ended, McSpadden criticized Bartlett for his lack of an educational funding plan.[29] In the first days of the session, Bartlett, who had campaigned on a platform of opposing new taxes, proposed to raise teacher salaries by a total of one thousand dollars over three years, with the increase to be funded from monies then allocated for county roads. This proposal infuriated teachers, who were angered by the paltriness of the proposal, and the county commissioners, who would lose road revenue. Despite Bartlett's furious opposition to a tax increase, the political climate was ripe for one, with the legislature reluctantly supporting an increase and the *Oklahoman* editorializing in favor of a higher sales tax.[30]

At the end of February, the legislature passed a bill calling for a five-hundred-dollar raise for teachers in 1968 and a similar raise in 1969, with the increase to be financed by a rise in cigarette and liquor taxes. Bartlett vetoed the measure. Oklahoma teachers, on the verge of striking, called for a one-day statewide teachers' rally to take place in Oklahoma City. On March 5, one day before the statewide meeting, the legislature and the governor agreed on a thirteen-hundred-dollar teacher pay increase over three years, paying for the raise with a five-cents-per-pack increase in cigarette taxes. This temporarily settled the salary issue, but the matter of teacher retirement remained unresolved and hotly debated until the end of the session. The rift with Governor Bartlett led Privett to tell a meeting of school administrators, "The chief executive thinks the school problem is solved for the next three years, but we legislators know better."[31]

Even with the distraction of the education crisis, the legislature still had to deal with other matters of governing the state, including legislation reestablishing a court system to comply with the voter-mandated court reforms. They set salaries for trial judges, establishing a pay scale for associate district judges that depended on the population of the county in which the judge sat. Some legislators were offended by the conduct of some of the Supreme Court justices, who personally lobbied legislators, especially lawyer-legislators, for pay raises for themselves.[32]

Legislators established the post of special district judge in counties with at least twenty-four thousand people, lowering the requirement from twenty-five thousand in order to accommodate the population of Canadian County. Special judges served at the pleasure of district judges, and their duties were limited.[33] The legislature also established a six-member Court of Appeals, composed of two three-member panels, as an intermediate appellate court for civil cases.[34] Since justices of the peace had been abolished, the legislature established a meaningful and efficient small claims procedure, authorizing court clerks to assist litigants with pleadings in order to avoid the burdensome cost of attorneys in small cases.[35] They barred judges from seeking any political office other than another judicial office, avoiding another incident like Judge Kirksey Nix's distasteful bid for attorney general a few years previously.[36]

Terms for district judges did not expire until 1970, and the legislation extended their terms until that time. The newly created position of associate district judge, however, was open for election in 1968. Sixty-nine county judges, whose jobs were abolished by the reform, filed for election as associate district judge; of those, forty-four were unopposed. Backers of the Sneed plan claimed this development demonstrated an inherent weakness of the legislative plan: the difficulty of getting rid of entrenched rural judges.[37]

The Sneed Plan Special Election

On September 17, four months after the 1968 legislature adjourned and more than a year after the submission of the initiative petition, State Question 441—the Sneed plan—finally made the Oklahoma ballot. After pointing out the high number of state questions already on the primary election ballot, Governor Bartlett ordered SQ 441 placed on the runoff ballot. As it happened, a runoff was necessary for only a few races, the most significant being for the Democratic nomination for Corporation Commission. Political forecasters therefore anticipated a light turnout.

Bartlett, calling both plans "excellent," announced his neutrality on SQ 441. Elsewhere in the state, the question drew heated debate. The *Oklahoman*, whose chief editorial writer, Clarke Thomas, had been instrumental in the plan's petition drive, printed editorials supporting the measure. The *Oklahoman* writers recalled Corn and Cargill's specious claims that bribes were campaign contributions and argued that, without judicial elections, no campaign contributions would be necessary. In a separate editorial, titled "Lest We Forget," the author called the scandal "the worst black eye Oklahoma ever had" and argued, "Courts must be established by laws that will absolutely prevent judges being bought like sheep."[38]

Endorsements for the Sneed plan came from newspapers, politicians, and the bar. The *Tribune* backed SQ 441, with its editorial writer asking where the "naysayer" lawyers critical of the questions were when "the little old ladies in tennis shoes [the League of Women Voters and PTA]" were circulating petitions to put the measure on the ballot.[39] Urban newspapers like the *Norman Transcript* and the *Oklahoma Journal* backed SQ 441, as did some rural papers, including the *Pawnee Chief*, the *Hughes County Times*, and the *Beaver Herald-Democrat*.[40] Former governor and campaigning U.S. Senate candidate Henry Bellmon backed the plan, risking the anger of Republican legislators like James Connor and Denzil Garrison during Bellmon's own Senate campaign. Former OU coach and U.S. Senate candidate Bud Wilkinson endorsed SQ 441 as well. Cleveland County district judge Elvin Brown wrote a strongly-worded memo to the local bar favoring the Sneed plan, arguing that increased judicial independence would make a judicial career more appealing to experienced lawyers.[41] The heads of Oklahoma's Roman Catholic and Episcopal Churches announced their support of the plan as well.[42]

The Sneed forces commissioned a poll, the results of which they released about two weeks prior to the election. Out of a sampling of six hundred voters, 50.7 percent claimed to be in favor of the Sneed plan, with only 24.7 percent opposed and the rest undecided. The plan seemed to be hugely popular in Tulsa, with 57.3 percent supporting the plan and only 15.7 percent opposed. In the rest of the state, voters claimed to favor the Sneed plan by margins varying from 54 percent to 46 percent.

Interestingly only 39.6 percent of those sampled claimed to have voted in the last judicial election; only 30 percent of that number knew for whom they had voted. Five percent felt their judge was "very honest," while another 52.7 percent thought their judge was "somewhat honest." Sixty-five percent claimed to be in favor of reform. Based on their own poll, the backers of SQ 411 therefore had great reason for optimism.[43]

However, the Sneed plan also encountered strong and vocal opposition. One of the leading critics was the *Tulsa World*, which editorialized against the plan several times. A week before the election, the *World* told its readers the plan "would vest all the power over Oklahoma's judiciary in the hands of the Supreme Court and its Chief Justice. That's too much power for any individual. . . . In truth, the plan voted by the people last year provides checks and balances on the court system, through the elected Oklahoma legislature." On the Sunday before the election, an editorial appearing on page one told readers, "Reform isn't limited to one idea. . . . Oklahoma has a plan approved by the Governor and the Legislature and the people."[44]

Republican legislators Denzil Garrison and James Connor, the Republican floor leaders of their respective houses, strongly campaigned against SQ 411. Garrison argued that rather than taking the politics out of the judiciary, the plan "merely concentrates the politics in a few hands." In Bartlesville, the hometown of both Garrison and Connor, the Washington County Republican and Democratic organizations bought adjoining advertisements in the *Bartlesville Examiner* opposing the state question. Four of Tulsa County's six district judges publicly opposed the Sneed plan, arguing the legislative plan should be granted an opportunity to work.[45]

The drafters of the Sneed plan had overlooked the state's industrial court, which heard workers' compensation cases. Adoption of SQ 411 therefore would have abolished the industrial court and forced those cases back to the district courts. Opponents of the Sneed plan gleefully jumped on this mistake, claiming the district courts would be overburdened. In a Tulsa debate with Leroy Blackstock, John McCune, the principal author of the legislative plan, mentioned this flaw in Sneed's proposal. For his part Blackstock emphasized the difficulty of ridding the system of substandard rural judges, pointing out that Bryan County judge Glenn Sharpe, who had become the first judge to be removed from office by the new Court on the Judiciary for accepting improper fees, had been unopposed for election.[46]

The electorate was voting for the second time in fifteen months on two remarkably similar proposals. After all, the legislative plan had been specifically created to deflect SQ 441, and each greatly changed the system that had existed since statehood. Although the plans had other differences, the voters would be called upon to decide two major issues. First, would the state's trial judges be selected by appointment or election? Second, would the legislature or the judiciary itself allocate and assign judicial resources?

On September 17 the voters answered those questions. Although they approved the other four major state questions on the ballot, Oklahomans overwhelmingly rejected the Sneed plan by a margin of 115,560 in favor to 171,620 opposed; only about 40 percent of those voting favored the question. SQ 441 carried only three counties: Oklahoma, Cleveland, and Payne. While Oklahoma County's support had been more than two to one in favor, the Sneed plan narrowly failed in Tulsa County. In some counties the vote was as much as ten to one against the Sneed plan.[47]

Sneed blamed the defeat in part on the unpopularity of the U.S. Supreme Court, then in the midst of a series of liberal rulings on constitutional criminal procedure. He also pointed out the progress made by the legislative plan, stating, "The legislative plan is so much superior to what we had in 1966." When asked if he would try to bring the matter back at a later time, Sneed replied, "Not at this time." The Sneed plan was dead.[48]

The Sneed plan failed for several reasons. First, the legislative plan had preempted the field. The electorate had, only fifteen months previously, adopted a new judicial framework. It made sense to see if it would work. Second, conservative Oklahomans, skeptical of government authority, questioned the wisdom of turning over judicial assignments and personnel to a largely unknown central body like the Oklahoma Supreme Court; the Supreme Court, of course, was the same entity whose shocking scandal had begun the process for reform in the first place. Third, the Sneed plan had nothing to offer rural Oklahomans, who opposed further centralization of the judiciary and weakening of rural legal authority.

The primary reason for the failure of the Sneed plan was simpler, though. Oklahomans, who had a political tradition of a long ballot with many elective offices, simply were unwilling to give up the right to elect local judges. The legislative plan, supported by nearly everyone in state government, had nearly fallen victim to the same problem. The electorate failed to see the correlation between electing judges and judicial corruption.

In September 1968 Chief Justice Jackson appointed Marian Opala as the state's first court administrator. Opala, a native of Poland, came to Oklahoma after enduring terrible suffering during World War II. A man of enormous intellect and energy, he had quietly assisted Senator Roy Grantham in the N. B. Johnson impeachment trial.[49] Opala now faced the formidable task of reorganizing the state's court system, centralizing its budgeting and personnel in Oklahoma City. Opala compared his job to being the executive director of a large corporation, with the board of directors being the state's nine Supreme Court justices and the other judges being shareholders. He later said, "When I took over as administrator there were 77 separate kingdoms, each independent, each comprising but one county, and it was difficult to recruit people for that new philosophy." His plans met resistance from judges in Tulsa, some judges in rural Oklahoma, and from court clerks, who had not previously been required to account to anyone but the voters for the court's money. He also met resistance from Republican officeholders, especially in northern Oklahoma, who rejected the nonpartisan approach of the new court system and resented what they saw as Democratic control.[50] Eventually judges and clerks became used to the new system, and the office of court administrator ran the business end of the judiciary.

The enactment of court reform had taken a circuitous route. On many occasions reform could have failed, and its eventual success was aided by several fortuitous events. The general public disgust with the court scandal certainly played a huge role, as did the embarrassing and obsolete justice of the peace system. McCarty's defeat was critical; it is hard to imagine a judicial nominating commission proposal passing the legislature with J. D. McCarty running the House of Representatives. Governor Bartlett held his ground with the legislature and insisted on the appointment of appellate judges; this would not have occurred had Bartlett not unexpectedly defeated Preston Moore in 1966. Finally, the energy of the Sneed plan backers in getting their proposal before the voters forced the legislature to propose a considerably stronger plan than the legislators otherwise would have passed.

At the time the Sneed plan failed, its backers saw the victory for the legislative plan as a win for the conservative legislature. Over time, though, it has become clear how far Oklahoma's judiciary came from 1963 through 1968. Oklahoma ridded itself of the justice of the peace system. The institution of the nonpartisan election of trial judges made the job more professional and less political. The establishment of the office of court administrator centralized court funding. The creation of the judicial nominating commission helped ensure that only qualified lawyers, not just political candidates, filled judicial vacancies. The question is not what Oklahoma could have done, but rather what it actually accomplished.

❖ 7
Oklahoma after Court Reform

Oklahoma's court reform system has now been in effect for more than fifty years. In two generations, more than enough time has elapsed to examine the strengths and weakness of the state's reformed judicial system. In this chapter I outline some of those strengths and weaknesses, beginning with the Court on the Judiciary.

The Court on the Judiciary

In 1968, two years after its establishment, the Court on the Judiciary removed Glenn Sharpe, a Bryan County judge who was found to have accepted nearly thirteen thousand dollars in exchange for approving marriage licenses. Sharpe fought his case all the way to the U.S. Supreme Court, unsuccessfully arguing that he was entitled to a jury trial, rather than a trial by eight sitting judges and one practicing attorney as authorized by the constitutional amendment. Sharpe's case established the authority of the Court on the Judiciary and ended any doubt about the legitimacy of its existence.[1]

However, a flaw in the system quickly became apparent. No statutory mechanism existed to investigate judicial complaints; a person with a grievance against a judge had no convenient agency charged with receiving the complaint and investigating its validity. In 1974 Senator Grantham authored a bill that established a Council on Judicial Complaints, which consisted of three attorneys. The Speaker of the House, the president pro tempore of the Senate, and the president of the Oklahoma Bar Association each had the responsibility of appointing one member of the body. The Council on Judicial Complaints immediately became very busy; in the first year of its existence, the council investigated thirty-six judicial complaints, dismissing nineteen of them.[2]

Grantham's legislation also directed that the Council on Judicial Complaints should operate in secrecy, a practice that the Oklahoma legislature strengthened in 1998. In addition to requiring that any proceedings of the Council on Judicial Complaints be held "in secrecy to the same extent as proceedings before a grand jury," Oklahoma's statute now requires a fine of up to one thousand dollars for witnesses or complainants who reveal to the public any information about the complaint. Additionally, judicial officers who reveal anything about judicial complaints are liable for a public reprimand by the Court on the Judiciary.[3]

This level of confidentiality is a two-edged sword. Demanding secrecy protects judges, whose credibility relies on public respect, from scurrilous and frivolous complaints. It also provides comfort to lawyers, court personnel, litigants, or other interested parties who wish to complain about a judge without fear of intimidation or public condemnation. However, something is draconian about requiring fines or judicial reprimands for those people who are simply reporting facts about the investigation of a public official. It also seems harsh to require silence from someone who believes to have been wronged and may violate the complainant's First Amendment right to free speech.

The Court on the Judiciary became very active in the 1970s and 1980s. In 1975 this court undertook the difficult case of Judge Bill Haworth, a district judge, former legislator, and longtime Muskogee political figure. After a fierce legal battle, the court found Haworth had operated a loan company from his judicial chambers, tampered with jury selection, and promised lenient treatment to a felon in exchange for political assistance to a candidate for district attorney. After Haworth was removed from the bench, he established a law practice with Gene Howard, the president pro tempore of the State Senate. He and Howard maintained a substantial criminal defense practice.[4]

In 1976 the court heard the case of Judge Sam Sullivan of Durant, another longtime local political figure who had been elected to the district court bench. Sullivan was accused of and ultimately found guilty of outlandish and abusive actions, including threatening to kill anyone who tried to have him disbarred or removed from office, saying escaped prisoners should have been killed, suggesting a couple kill their son and throw his body into a lake, jailing a litigant for not knowing his Social Security number, and holding a contempt hearing against a bailiff and refusing to allow him to have an attorney. After the Court on the Judiciary removed Sullivan and disqualified him from further judicial office, he unsuccessfully ran for election as district attorney, even though he was the subject of a pending disbarment case.[5]

In that same year, the court tried Gar Graham, an associate district judge from Oklahoma County. Graham had publicly feuded with nearly everyone in the Oklahoma County courthouse, using the press to vent his complaints about other judges. He also clashed with the legislature, eventually posting a sign outside his courtroom door banning lawyer-legislators from practicing in his courtroom. The court suspended Graham for four months without pay and ordered him publicly reprimanded but did not remove him from office.

The common thread of the Haworth, Sullivan, and Graham cases is continued participation in partisan politics by sitting judges. Haworth, Sullivan, and Graham all viewed their positions as judges as vehicles with which to wield political power, not to adjudicate disputes. The reforms of the 1960s had made it clear that judges were to act as independent interpreters of the law, not as advocates for themselves or other partisan or personal interests. Eventually, cases of political interference by judges dwindled after the 1970s. Judges who saw themselves as partisan political figures or saw the bench as a stepping-stone for nonjudicial political office began disappearing. Litigants gradually came to see courthouses as places where they could expect fair treatment, regardless of who their lawyer was or that person's political persuasion or station in life. The Oklahoma bench was no longer a place for political power-brokering.

Not all cases ended in conviction. In 1977 Judge Elvin Brown, a hardworking but autocratic district judge from Norman, went before the Court on the Judiciary. Brown was accused of using his office to oppress the prosecution in criminal cases, inappropriate language, and intimidating behavior. Brown was acquitted, becoming to this date the only judge to come before the court not to be sanctioned in some way.[6]

The Court on the Judiciary also began to use its constitutionally authorized power of compulsory retirement to force judges off the bench. With this less onerous tool, which allowed the court to retire judges with "a mental or physical disability preventing the proper performance of official duty, or incompetence to perform the duties of the office," the court retired several judges whose health issues had clouded their ability to do their jobs. These included, in 1971, Kirksey Nix, the former state senator who had run for attorney general without resigning his judgeship, and in 1988, Joe Cannon, a former legislator and aide to Governor Edmondson who had served controversially as an Oklahoma County district judge for a number of years. Cannon accepted the medical retirement shortly before facing trial before the court on charges of gross partiality.[7] In 1994 the court approved the medical retirement of Judge Melinda Monnet of Oklahoma County, who, although only thirty-three years old, claimed numerous job-related illnesses, exhibited strange and inappropriate behavior on the bench, and had not appeared for work in several months.[8]

By 2002 the Court on the Judiciary had removed six judges, suspended three, retired eleven, and one had resigned before trial. Since that year, no judges have been removed by action of the Court on the Judiciary; no trials have even taken place. That does not mean, however, that judges have not been subject to discipline. In 2004 Judge Donald Thompson resigned shortly before trial in the Court on the Judiciary after being accused of bizarre and abusive sexual behavior on the bench and in the courthouse. Thompson later was convicted and sentenced to prison. In 2005 Judge Steve Lile of the Court of Criminal Appeals became the only appellate judge since court reform to be forced out of office by scandal. Lile, who had filed false travel expense claims and abused his judicial authority in order to help his incarcerated son, was later disbarred. Two other judges, Tammy Bass-Lesure and Wayne Olmstead, resigned rather than face the Court on the Judiciary; both eventually pled guilty or no contest to crimes.[9] Several special district judges have been terminated or forced to resign over the years; however, these judges are appointed officials and are subject to firing by district judges, without the involvement of the Court on the Judiciary.

After several quiet years, the Court on the Judiciary became active again in 2018. Oklahoma chief justice Douglas Combs filed a removal petition against District Judge Curtis DeLapp of Washington County. DeLapp was charged with numerous abuses of judicial power. These included, among other things, holding people in contempt of court for frivolous reasons, then refusing to allow those people to have a hearing. He also allegedly locked latecomers to court out of the courtroom, then issued warrants for their arrest for failure to appear for court, even though he knew that they had simply been tardy. Less than three weeks after the charges were filed, DeLapp resigned his post.[10]

The Court on the Judiciary has worked well. The bar and the Supreme Court have been careful about abusing the power of the Court on the Judiciary, using its power only in the most egregious and thoroughly investigated cases. The bench and bar respect the Court on the Judiciary, and its existence serves as an effective deterrent to judges who may be tempted to violate the rules.

The Judicial Nominating Commission and Judicial Selection

In recent years the concept of the Judicial Nominating Commission has come under serious fire, especially from conservative Republican legislators. The Supreme Court has declared several legislative acts unconstitutional, including tort reform measures that had broad legislative support. It also ordered the removal from the state capitol grounds of a statue displaying the Ten Commandments. The Supreme Court has also strictly interpreted, sometimes confusingly, a constitutional requirement that legislation be restricted to only one subject and has struck down antiabortion legislation. These and other court actions have angered some members of the legislature.

The legislature has repeatedly considered giving more power in judicial appointments to the governor and legislature and less to the Judicial Nominating Commission. During the winter of 2010–2011, an incident involving a Supreme Court vacancy saw the relationship between the legislature and the committee deteriorate substantially. In October 2010 longtime Supreme Court justice Marian Opala died. In November, voters approved changes to the makeup of the Judicial Nominating Commission and also elected Republican Mary Fallin to replace outgoing Democrat Brad Henry as governor. Fallin's term was to begin in January. Over furious Republican protests, who wanted to fill the seat after the constitutional changes to the committee had become effective and Fallin had been inaugurated, the Judicial Nominating Committee quickly took applications and recommended three candidates to Governor Henry. Three days before his term ended, Henry appointed Judge Noma Gurich to the post.[11]

A 2010 constitutional amendment changed the number of people on the Judicial Nominating Commission to fifteen members. Of those fifteen members, six are to be appointed by the governor. None of those six may be members of the Oklahoma Bar Association (OBA) or have any immediate family who are OBA members, and those six gubernatorial appointees must be divided equally by party. Six lawyer members are elected by the Oklahoma Bar Association. Three at-large members fill out the balance of the commission—one selected by the president pro tempore of the Senate, one by the Speaker of the House, and one by the commission members. The same rules of bar membership and party allocation apply to those three slots; no more than two of those three can be members of the same party. At least nine of the fifteen members, therefore, must be nonlawyers, and those members may not have a lawyer licensed in any state in the immediate family.[12] This appears to be a positive change. While input from lawyers is important in selecting judges, it is also vital that the qualifications of aspiring judges be viewed by impartial outsiders, and that the public not have the perception that judges are selected by an exclusive group of lawyers.

In April 2019 the Oklahoma legislature passed legislation changing the demographic allocation of Oklahoma Supreme Court seats. Historically, the Supreme Court has comprised nine districts, with each district being allowed one seat. This has resulted in geographic imbalance. Supreme Court District Three, the Oklahoma County seat, has 41 percent of the state's lawyers and 10 percent of the state's population, while District Two, in southeastern Oklahoma, has only 2.5 percent of the attorneys and less than 9 percent of the population. The 2019 legislation allocates one Supreme Court seat for each of Oklahoma's five congressional districts, with the other four seats to be appointed from the state at large.[13]

In the two generations since 1967, it is hardly surprising that political and legal thinking on the subject of judicial selection has evolved. In 2002 the U.S. Supreme Court changed the playing field for judicial candidates with its decision in *Republican Party of Minnesota v. White*.[14] In a 5-4 decision authored by Justice Antonin Scalia, the court held that Minnesota's provision prohibiting political candidates from announcing their views on disputed legal and political issues violated the candidate's First Amendment right to free speech. This opened the doors for candidates for elected judicial office to announce their positions on issues that would come before them as judges.

Although *Republican Party of Minnesota v. White* is admittedly now long-established law, it still seems to this writer to have been a serious mistake. Judicial candidates are now free to run for office on platforms such as being hard on drug offenders or taking a hard line against insurance companies or personal injury plaintiffs. Assuming, for example, a judge has been elected on a platform of being favorable to defendants and insurance companies in personal injury cases, plaintiffs will feel uncomfortable about appearing in front of that judge and skeptical about the idea of fair treatment in that judge's court. This problem is exacerbated by the U.S. Supreme Court's ruling in *Citizens United v. Federal Election Commission,* which bars the government from restricting independent political expenditures, opening the door for those with a stake in judicial races to spend massive amounts of money on judicial campaigns.[15]

In recent years, judicial selection has become a subject of serious study for political scientists. Distinguished government scholars James L. Gibson, Chris W. Bonneau, and Melinda Gann Hall all make forceful and persuasive arguments in favor of partisan judicial elections, in which the candidates identify themselves by political party. They reason that judges, like legislators, are public officeholders, whose decisions should reflect the values of the community in which they serve. The candidate's party affiliation, according to them, gives the voter some information regarding the potential judge's ideology and positions on the issues. Gibson, Bonneau, and Hall believe that the public benefits from expensive, partisan judicial races, which help educate the public on their judges and ensure that judges rule as their constituents expect.[16]

Professor Gibson, responding to an article titled "Why Judicial Elections Stink" by Charles Gardner Geyh, colorfully compared judicial elections to anchovies on a Caesar salad, pointing out that this may ruin the salad for some people while enhancing its enjoyment for others. Gibson concludes, "Still, for most constituents of courts, the predominant essence of judicial elections is not foul. Because it is not, holding judges accountable, with its messiness and fuss, still serves to make courts more legitimate and hence more efficacious, which cannot help but bolster democracy and the rule of law."[17]

On the other hand, Fordham professor Jed Handelsman Shugerman argues strongly for merit selection of judges.[18] Shugerman states, "In this particular moment in American history, the two biggest threats to judicial independence are money and job security. . . . Of the most realistic models, merit selection . . . turns out to address both the problems. . . . The merit system's most concrete advantages are that it shifts the balance to judicial independence from the influence of party politics and that it has produced more job security for its judges."[19]

Pro-election scholars like Gibson, Bonneau, and Hall make good points. Within the boundaries of the laws and reason, judges should reflect the values of the communities in which they serve. Also, to some extent, a candidate's party affiliation can provide an indication of the potential judge's philosophy on political and legal issues.

However, I believe firmly that the disadvantages of partisan elections far outweigh their advantages. Judges and legislators have entirely different governmental roles. Legislators are expected to represent their district in the legislature, making sure that the best interests and desires of their constituents are represented in the state legislative body and reflected in legislation. Judges, on the other hand, have a duty to analyze the facts of the case at hand and apply the law to those facts. Judges should not make decisions based on what is best for a locality or what result the judge's constituents want. A judge who simply responds to public opinion without considering the facts and the applicable law is not doing the job of a judge. Judicial independence is a fundamental part of the American legal system, and it must be preserved.

Advocates of partisan judicial elections, especially at the statewide appellate level, should take careful note of what happened in a contested appellate judge election in West Virginia. In 2002 a West Virginia jury found A. T. Massey Coal Company, a large local coal mining company led by Don Blankenship, liable for fraud and awarded the plaintiffs $50 million in damages. Massey took the case to the West Virginia Supreme Court of Appeals. In 2004 a partisan judicial election occurred, and Republican Brent Benjamin challenged Democratic incumbent Warren McGraw.

Blankenship, whose case was pending before the court, formed a political organization called "And for the Sake of the Kids" and donated almost $2.5 million to the organization. The organization then ran advertisements calling incumbent Warren McGraw "radical" and "too dangerous for our kids." Blankenship also spent more than five hundred thousand dollars on direct mailings and letters soliciting donations and television and newspaper advertising supporting Benjamin's campaign and viciously criticizing McGraw. Blankenship spent more on the election than the committees of the two candidates combined and more than three times the amount spent by Benjamin's own committee. As Chief Justice John Roberts pointed out in his eventual dissent on the case, a group called Consumers for Justice spent about $2 million in support of McGraw. Benjamin won the election and became a member of West Virginia's five-member Supreme Court of Appeals.

The plaintiff asked Benjamin to recuse himself from hearing the case. After deliberating for about six months, Benjamin denied the motion but stated that he found "no objective information" that he had prejudged the case, had a bias for or against any litigant, or that he would be anything but fair and impartial. In 2007, by a three-to-two vote, the court reversed the earlier finding, setting aside the $50 million verdict; Justice Benjamin voted with the majority, in favor of Massey Coal.

Shortly thereafter, photos surfaced of one of the other two justices who had voted in Massey's favor, Justice Elliott Maynard, vacationing on the French Riviera with none other than Don Blankenship, an inconvenient fact neither Maynard nor Blankenship had previously disclosed.[20] Maynard recused, as did another justice who had been publicly critical of both Benjamin and Blankenship, leaving two slots out of five open. Benjamin, who by then was the court's chief justice, appointed two justices to fill the vacancies and rehear the case. In April 2008 the West Virginia court again reversed the jury's verdict, once again by a three-to-two decision with Benjamin again providing the deciding vote in favor of Massey.[21]

The case eventually went to the U.S. Supreme Court. In a five-to-four decision, the Supreme Court, in an opinion written by Justice Kennedy, held that Benjamin's refusal to recuse himself violated the Due Process clause of the Constitution. Chief Justice Roberts dissented, joined by Justices Alito, Thomas, and Scalia. Justice Roberts argued the majority had opened a Pandora's box on the question of judicial recusal, listing forty separate questions not raised by the majority decision with which justices may now have to deal. Scalia also wrote a separate opinion, accusing the majority of continuing "its quixotic quest to right all wrongs and repair all imperfections through the Constitution" and agreeing with Roberts that the majority had simply added confusion to the issue.[22]

The *Massey* case embodies all that is wrong with partisan judicial elections, especially at the appellate level, where statewide law is made. In a race for the highest court in a relatively small state, two nonprofit corporations spent $5 million attempting to get their candidate into office. One of those corporations was financed by someone with a direct interest in a case pending before that court, while the other was funded by attorneys with regular business there. When Justice Benjamin won, he twice cast the deciding vote in favor of the party who had donated $3 million to his campaign. It took a five-to-four decision of the U.S. Supreme Court to correct such an obvious miscarriage of justice.[23]

In Texas, Oklahoma's neighbor to the south, judicial campaigns, especially for civil appellate positions, are extremely politicized and expensive. Beginning in the 1980s, donations from trial lawyers, ranchers, and other interests of over $100,000 to judicial campaigns became commonplace. This led to an ugly incident in which Houston trial lawyer Joe Jamail, who represented Pennzoil in an important contractual case against Texaco, donated $10,000 to the judge hearing the case. The judge issued several rulings in Pennzoil's favor, and Jamail won a $10.5 billion verdict against Texaco. While the case was on appeal, Jamail donated $355,000 to Texas Supreme Court justices, and the Supreme Court upheld the verdict, eventually forcing Texaco into bankruptcy court. Jamail subsequently collected a fee of between $330 million and $420 million.[24] Texas Supreme Court races, now completely dominated by Republicans, remain expensive and subject to large campaign donations.

In 2018 Wisconsin experienced a wildly expensive Supreme Court election between trial judges Rebecca Dallet, a liberal, and Michael Screnock, a conservative. Although Wisconsin's judicial elections are officially nonpartisan, the race quickly became a contest along party lines. One ultimately unsuccessful candidate, who was defeated in the primary election, argued, "A nonpartisan judiciary is a fairy tale, and it always has been."

The race was the first statewide election since Donald Trump had unexpectedly carried Wisconsin in 2016. Dallet, who used Trump as an issue in her campaign, received endorsements from former vice president Joe Biden and Senator Cory Booker, and former attorney general Eric Holder, none of whom are Wisconsin residents. The National Rifle Association and the Wisconsin Republican Party endorsed Screnock in what supposedly was a nonpartisan race. At least $2.6 million went toward television advertising. In the end Dallet won easily, but the race was seen as a win for Democrats, not as a nonpartisan judicial election.[25]

If we are to have judicial elections, especially at the statewide appellate level, it is worth discussing how to finance them in a political and legal climate in which the freedom to spend money is equated with free speech. As noted earlier, judicial elections are down-ballot races, meaning that they rarely draw the public interest that contests for governor, attorney general, and other high-profile offices do. Other than friends and family members of the candidate, there are four likely sources of donations: insurance companies, plaintiffs' personal injury attorneys, large corporations, and other attorneys, especially large law firms. All these potential contributors have considerable business before the courts, creating inherent conflicts for judges who have received contributions. When one of the attorneys or parties has contributed to a judge's campaign, it is difficult or impossible to see how the judicial playing field can be level; it is even harder to imagine a litigant who has lost a case to a contributor thinking he has received fair treatment. The drawbacks to appellate judicial elections far outweigh the advantages.

The Retention Ballot and Nonpartisan Trial Judge Elections

Oklahoma voters adopted the retention ballot for appellate judges in 1967. Since that time, no Oklahoma appellate judges have been unseated by the voters; all have been retained. In the first judicial retention election in 1968, the Oklahoma Bar Association endorsed the retention of the three Supreme Court justices on the ballot but opposed a new term for the controversial

Judge Kirksey Nix of the Court of Criminal Appeals. Nix bought advertising, responded in the press, and was retained by the voters.[26] Since then, the bar has taken a hands-off approach to retention of specific judges.

Generally, judges on the retention ballot average about 60 percent voter approval. In 2018, all twelve appellate judges won retention. Judge Barbara Swinton of the Court of Civil Appeals and Judge Dana Kuehn of the Court of Criminal Appeals led the field with 64 percent approval, while Supreme Court justice James Edmondson, whose brother, Drew, was the Democratic nominee for governor, received the lowest retention percentage, 59 percent. In 2016 Justice Jim Winchester, who received the most votes for retention, received 61 percent voter approval, while the lowest, Justice Douglas L. Combs, received 58 percent. In 2014, nine justices and appellate judges were on Oklahoma's retention ballot. The lowest-performing judge, Justice John Reif, received 59 percent of the votes to retain him; the highest-performing judge, Justice Tom Colbert, received 62 percent.

Nationwide, judicial retention remains very high, and Oklahoma's experience is relatively consistent with other states with the same system. Between 1936 and 2009, 637 state Supreme Court justices faced retention votes; eight lost. However, in 2010, Iowa voters, disgruntled by a Supreme Court decision that made Iowa the first state to legalize same-sex marriage, voted out of office three judges who supported the decision. In that same year, hotly contested judicial retention votes took place in Alaska, Colorado, Florida, Illinois, and Michigan, with all the incumbents being retained in office.[27]

The issue therefore is whether the judicial retention ballot is an effective tool with which to judge judicial performance. In Oklahoma the average voter, who has little to no experience with the courts and even less with appellate courts, has no frame of reference with which to determine the performance of a particular judge. While some states have some mechanism for judicial evaluation, Oklahoma does not. Certainly over more than a half-century Oklahoma has had some appellate judges who did not deserve to remain on the bench, but the electorate has no way of learning whether judges are doing a good job.[28]

Oklahomans now have more than fifty years of electing trial judges on a nonpartisan ballot. With some exceptions, the system has mostly run smoothly. In rural areas of the state, it is relatively common for judges, especially incumbents, to be unopposed; after all, the potential talent is limited to lawyers living in the judicial district, which may be a relatively low number. In contested elections the incumbent unquestionably has a significant advantage, although this is probably no more true in judicial elections than state legislative or U.S. congressional elections.

In 2018, three Oklahoma County district judges and one Tulsa County district judge were defeated for reelection. The Tulsa County judge was the subject of an investigation into his patronage of a massage parlor. One of the Oklahoma County judges, Howard R. Haralson, heard a bitter and controversial divorce between billionaire oilman Harold Hamm and his wife, Sue Ann, now Arnall. Ms. Arnall donated one hundred thousand dollars to a super PAC that targeted Haralson for defeat. Haralson was defeated in the primary.[29]

In the 2014 election, 98 percent of all incumbent trial judges in Oklahoma retained their office. One hundred eight candidates were unopposed. Three judges were voted out. Two of those three defeated candidates had been appointed to the bench and thus faced the voters for the first time. In 2010 at least three long-serving incumbent judges were unseated.[30]

I served for twenty-eight years as associate district judge of Carter County, Oklahoma, a county with a population of approximately fifty thousand people. I served seven terms and was never opposed for election until I opted not to be a candidate in 2014. I can therefore claim some expertise in the field of nonpartisan judicial elections, although without question my objectivity is compromised by my own experience. In my view, Oklahoma's establishment of nonpartisan elections for trial judges was then and still remains a healthy concept. Like any other officeholder, judges must be accountable for the way they conduct their office. Judicial elections, including nonpartisan ones, are always, as one California judge said, "the crocodile in the bathtub," that is, constantly on the mind of the officeholder.[31] Prudent incumbent judges therefore take pains to explain controversial and unpopular decisions, preferably in writing. It is unfair and unacceptable to tie judicial decisions to political parties; as I argued earlier, legislators and judges have completely different duties. However, everyone, including judges, should have someone to whom to answer.

From my observation, most Oklahomans respect their state judicial system. They realize every case is different, and sometimes the expected result does not occur. They understand that judges are bound by the law. Most litigants understand that, unlike legislators, judges are barred from discussing their cases with them without the other side being present. However, they also believe that they have the right to be treated courteously and respectfully by judges and their staffs, that cases should move expeditiously, and that judicial decisions should be made openly and not behind closed doors or for political reasons.

The Results of Reform and the Factors in Its Passage

The Oklahoma Supreme Court scandal exposed significant deficiencies in Oklahoma's judicial network. The system encouraged favoritism and doing business through the back door. Litigants were in danger of having their cases decided on who their lawyer was, not the merits of their case. In the last half-century, the legal industry has become considerably more professional in this aspect; although some ex parte communication no doubt occurs, it is now the rare exception, not the rule.

The judiciary has also become considerably more professional. Judges are no longer identified by political party, so they are not seen as just some more political office-seekers. Most judges see their office as separate from other political positions. While they may seek to move up the judicial ladder, it is a rare judge who sees his or her job as a gateway to nonjudicial political office. The existence of the Judicial Nominating Commission for appellate judgeships and midterm trial vacancies also increases the professionalism of the judiciary as well as public faith in the courts.

The absence of a meaningful way to discipline judges certainly helped contribute to the bribery and corruption scandal. Until it was finally exposed, corruption in the Supreme Court had been rumored for years. However, no convenient or practical mechanism for investigating complaints or removing judges had existed. The establishment of the Court on the Judiciary cured this problem. In addition to accountability to the voters, judges realize that they must behave professionally and responsibly.

Conclusion

In writing the state's constitution, Oklahoma's founders relied on their southern and Populist philosophies, which, among other things, led to the creation of an inordinate number of elected offices. These political concepts, along with the state's relative poverty, led to a government on the cheap that was not responsive to the needs of its citizens. Oklahoma's legal structure of its first fifty years featured a politicized and inefficient judiciary, lack of prosecutorial resources, the ineffective county attorney system, a dearth of statewide law enforcement officials, the scandalous justice of the peace system, and the confusing and incomprehensible trial court framework. It also led to appointment or election of at least three, and almost certainly more, corrupt Supreme Court justices who accepted bribes and allowed undue, backdoor influence by dishonest, power-brokering lawyers and businessmen. No mechanism existed to investigate allegations of wrongdoing, and once the corruption was exposed, no satisfactory procedures were in place to investigate or prosecute the offenders.

A number of factors led to the exposure of the scandal. The huge amount of money offered by Hugh Carroll and accepted by N. S. Corn involved so many people and was so suspicious that discovery of the crime became easier, if not inevitable. Although corruption on the court had been rumored for many years, the *Selected Investments* case simply was too big and complicated to keep quiet forever. Nevertheless, without the persistence of determined authorities who continued to look into Corn's tangled finances and the Selected Investments bankruptcy, the scandal may never have been exposed.

The scandal occurred at a time when the Republican Party was finally gaining a foothold in Oklahoma politics. Although their numbers in the legislature were still small, those Republicans who were in office consistently advocated for reform. Without G. T. Blankenship's courageous publication of Corn's statement on the House floor, it is hard to say what would have happened, but the chances of a Democratic legislature choosing to challenge Speaker McCarty on such an incendiary issue seem slim. Governor Bellmon, the state's first Republican governor, made sure the scandal remained in the public eye and helped force Welch and Johnson from the bench. Governor Bartlett remained steadfast in his advocacy of the Judicial Nominating Commission and retention voting for appellate judges. Without Bartlett's tenacity, neither the commission nor retention voting would have become a reality.

The electorate also played a significant role. Since the election of J. Howard Edmondson in the 1958 gubernatorial election, voters had demonstrated their impatience with the insider-friendly politics of the state's first half-century. The next two elected governors were Republicans; one of the issues in Bartlett's 1966 campaign against Preston Moore was court reform. Against all odds, the voters in J. D. McCarty's reapportioned legislative district unseated the powerful Speaker, who was encountering legal troubles of his own. Had McCarty remained Speaker, court reform, if it occurred at all, would have taken a considerably different and less comprehensive form. The reapportioned legislature of 1967 was considerably different from legislatures of previous years and less entrenched in the politics of the past.

In their development of the 1967 court reform plan, the state's leaders demonstrated leadership, political skill, and bipartisan ability to compromise. Spurred by the necessity of court reform but wary of the far-reaching Sneed plan, the legislative leadership and governor created a plan palatable to the state's conservative voters. They set the proposal for a special election, which drew voters educated on the issue and motivated to express their opinion. Even with the advantages the authorities gave to the propositions, they still only narrowly met with the voters' approval, demonstrating the political acuity of the authors of the reforms.

Finally, the Oklahoma bar deserves credit for helping to create the atmosphere that led to the enactment of reform. Humiliated and mortified by the corruption in their ranks, most lawyers pitched in to try to ensure that a catastrophic event like the Supreme Court scandal would not happen again. The federal officials who doggedly pursued the original investigation were lawyers. The principals in the legislature's movement to impeach Welch and Johnson and negotiate and enact the judicial reform plan were lawyer-legislators. The leadership of the Oklahoma Bar Association took a very active role in investigating the scandal, preparing the reform plan, and persuading the voters to adopt it. Although his reform proposal never became law, Earl Sneed's activism on the issue of court reform gave urgency and energy to the crisis in the court system. Without pressure from the Sneed plan, legislative reform would have been much less extensive.

Oklahoma is once again a one-party state. As of 2018, all statewide offices and overwhelming majorities of both houses of the legislature are occupied by Republicans. Republicans hold both seats in the U.S. Senate and four of the five congressional posts. In the absence of a healthy Democratic Party, the state is in danger of falling victim to the same problems it had fifty years ago: factionalism, lack of voter interest, absence of a viable loyal opposition, and domination by incumbents.

Oklahoma's judicial system is by no means perfect. Judicial decision making is an inexact science subject to critical interpretation, and much of it is subjective and discretionary. However, Oklahoma's reforms have led to an experienced, professional judiciary, in which a judge is no longer considered just another party official. Instead, most Oklahomans consider their judges to be independent of special interests and seekers of appropriate results to litigation. The credit for this outcome belongs to the reformers of the 1960s.

Notes

Chapter 1

1. William A. Berry and James Edwin Alexander, *Justice for Sale: The Shocking Scandal of the Oklahoma Supreme Court* (Oklahoma City: Macedon, 1996), 36–39; *Daily Oklahoman*, January 22, 1965, p. 3.
2. Berry and Alexander, *Justice for Sale*, 39.
3. V. O. Key Jr., *Southern Politics in State and Nation* (1949; reprint, Knoxville: University of Tennessee Press, 1984), 387–88.
4. James R. Scales and Danney Goble, *Oklahoma Politics: A History* (Norman: University of Oklahoma Press, 1982). The authors based much of their analysis of earlier Oklahoma politics on Scales's 1949 University of Oklahoma PhD dissertation, "Political History in Oklahoma."
5. Scales and Goble, *Oklahoma Politics*, 118–54.
6. Richard D. Bingham, *Reapportionment of the Oklahoma House of Representatives: Politics and Process* (Norman, OK: Legislative Research Series, Bureau of Government Research, 1972), 2–3.
7. Linda D. Wilson, "Grant County," *The Encyclopedia of Oklahoma History and Culture*, https://www.okhistory.org./publications/enc/entry/php?;entry=GR009 (accessed December 29, 2019). The 2010 census lists Grant County's population at 4,527, about one-quarter of the population claimed one hundred years earlier.
8. Larkin Warner, "Oklahoma Economy," *The Encyclopedia of Oklahoma History and Culture*, https://www.okhistory.org/publications/enc/entry/php?entry=OK041 (accessed December 29, 2019).
9. U.S. Bureau of the Census, 1960 Census of Population, "Advance Reports, Final Population Counts," November 30, 1960, www2.census.gov/library/publications/decennial/1960/population-pc-a1/15611126ch4.pdf, p. 83.
10. Scales and Goble, *Oklahoma Politics*, 36.
11. J. S. Cockburne, *A History of English Assizes, 1558–1714* (Cambridge: Cambridge University Press, 1927), 155–76.
12. This occurred in the case of Paul Powers, an Oklahoma County JP who was forced to resign (*Oklahoman*, February 17, 1965, p. 4).
13. Governor Henry Bellmon to Bill Johnson (Hobart businessman), May 28, 1965, Henry Louis Bellmon Papers (hereafter Bellmon Papers), Box 39, File 6, Oklahoma State University, Stillwater.
14. Clarence Callender, *American Courts: Their Organization and Procedure* (New York: McGraw-Hill, 1972), 52–53.
15. Chester H. Smith, "The Justices of the Peace System in the United States," *California Law Review* 15 (1927): 118–41.

16. Sir Thomas Skyrme, *History of Justice of the Peace*, vol. 3 (Chichester, UK: Countrywide Press, 1991), 125.
17. As of 1965, fourteen states had abolished the office of justice of the peace (*The Justice of the Peace Today*, New York University study [New York: Institute of Judicial Administration, 1965], 2).
18. Ibid., 2–3.
19. Karen E. Kalius, interview with Marian P. Opala (hereafter Opala interview), June 9, 2009, Marian P. Opala archives, Oklahoma Hall of Fame, Oklahoma City, Oklahoma (hereafter Opala archives).
20. Bob Burke and Ryan Leonard, *Opala: In Faithful Service to the Law* (Oklahoma City: Oklahoma Heritage Association, 2012), 130–31.
21. Opala interview.
22. *Oklahoman*, January 3, 1956, p. 5.
23. In a 1933 speech, Oklahoma Supreme Court justice Fletcher Riley had described Oklahoma as "the most litigious place in the English-speaking world." Whether this statement was literally true or not, the Oklahoma courts certainly were busy (*Oklahoman*, August 30, 1933, p. 4).
24. Scales and Goble, *Oklahoma Politics*, 103.
25. In 1915 the number of justices had been increased from five to nine.
26. In 1932, for example, about eleven hundred civil appeals were filed with the Supreme Court, or approximately five every working day (Justice Fletcher Riley, quoted in *Oklahoman*, August 30, 1933, p. 4).
27. The United States is one of only a very few countries that hold elections for judges. Legal historians have generally attributed the practice of judicial elections to the 1830s Andrew Jackson era, with its emphasis on the common man and distrust of large institutions. Historian Jed Handelsman Shugerman, however, convincingly argues that the concept of judicial elections evolved from state citizenry, often acting through constitutional conventions, seeking judicial independence from coercion and retaliation by state governors and legislatures for courtroom decisions with which the officials disagreed (*The People's Courts: Pursuing Judicial Independence in America* [Cambridge, MA: Harvard University Press], 2012).
28. James R. Scales, a future president of Oklahoma Baptist University and Wake Forest University, pointed this out very eloquently and persuasively in his 1949 University of Oklahoma doctoral dissertation (Scales and Goble, *Oklahoma Politics*, 50–51).
29. Philip Simpson, "The Modernization and Reform of the Oklahoma Judiciary," *Oklahoma Politics* (October 1994): 1–4.
30. Jack N. Hays, "Selection of Judges in Oklahoma," *Tulsa Law Review* 2 (1965): 127–35.
31. Judith Maute, *Peevyhouse v. Garland Coal & Mining Co. Revisited: The Ballad of Willie and Lucille*, Northwestern University Law Review 89 (1995): 1341–478.
32. *Oklahoma Law Review* 4 (1951): 251–65. The ABA standards had been published in 1937, fourteen years prior to the OU study.
33. *Oklahoman*, June 22, 1954, p. 16; February 29, 1944, p. 13. Dozens of similar advertisements appeared in the *Oklahoman* during this period.
34. *Oklahoman*, November 7, 1948, p. 24. At that time the population of northwest Oklahoma City was almost exclusively white. Nearly all African Americans lived in the northeastern areas of the city.

NOTES TO CHAPTER 1   133

35. *Oklahoman*, January 26, 1947, p. 33.
36. Letter from Banking Commissioner O. B. Mothersead to Governor Johnston Murray, February 1, 1951, Johnston Murray Papers (hereafter Johnston Murray Papers), Box 1, Folder 12, Oklahoma Department of Libraries.
37. Robert L. Dorman, *Alfalfa Bill: A Life in Politics* (Norman: University of Oklahoma Press, 2018); Keith L. Bryant, *Alfalfa Bill Murray* (Norman: University of Oklahoma Press, 1968), 151–72.
38. Erin Dowell, "Murray, Johnston," *The Encyclopedia of Oklahoma History and Culture*, https: www.okhistory.org/publications/enc/entry.php?entry=MU013 (accessed December 31, 2019).
39. Otis Sullivant, *Oklahoman*, June 19, 1950, p. 1.
40. Scales and Goble, *Oklahoma Politics*, 267–68.
41. *Oklahoman*, August 28, 1958, p. 1.
42. Selected Investments was not licensed by the federal Securities and Exchange Commission. Its only license came from the state of Oklahoma (*Oklahoman*, December 24, 1957, p. 1).
43. Although Carroll, who was not a member of the legislature, was allowed to speak before the committee, two representatives who were not committee members were not initially allowed to speak against it.
44. *Oklahoman*, May 10, 1951, p. 8.
45. *Oklahoman*, May 19, 1951, p. 1.
46. Cope, by then a semiretired private attorney, continued to hector Murray with demands that he resume the probe. Murray answered Cope's letters but continuously found funding or personnel reasons to explain the investigation's stall. Letters from Cope to Murray and Murray's responses, January 1, 1952; January 9, 1952; February 27, 1952; February 29, 1952. A notation on the bottom of one of Cope's letters bears the pencil notation, "Tuesday, April 8, 1952 at 11:00 A.M." It is unclear whether a meeting took place (Johnston Murray Papers, 8-N-1-1, Box 21, Folder 14, Oklahoma Department of Libraries).
47. The author's father, William L. Card, was a member of the 1951 legislature.
48. *Oklahoman*, December 24, 1957, p. 1.
49. *Oklahoman*, January 9, 1958, p. 8; February 18, 1958, p. 1.
50. Testimony of Julia Carroll, *United States v. Carroll*, Vol. 4, p. 184, United States Archives, Fort Worth, Texas.
51. Cargill's father, although poor when Cargill was a child, became a successful physician later in life.
52. O. A. Cargill, *My First 80 Years* (Oklahoma City: Banner Books, 1965), 1–29.
53. The *Oklahoman* quoted Cargill as claiming he had brandished a pistol at the Logan County officers (*Oklahoman*, August 30, 1920, p. 1).
54. Bobby Dobbs, "1920 Lynching of Claude Chandler: Shedding Light on a Painful Past," *Oklahoman*, February 21, 2016, p. 1A.
55. Scales and Goble, *Oklahoma Politics*, 106–34.
56. *Oklahoman*, July 7, 1926, p. 1; July 8, 1926, p. 1; July 10, 1926, p. 1. Cargill publicly identified himself with the Klan on some occasions and denied it on others. The *Daily Oklahoman* clearly identified Cargill as a Klansman in its July 22, 1926, edition.

57. *Oklahoman,* October 12, 1939, p. 1; October 13, 1939, p. 1; October 14, 1939, p. 1; October 15, 1939, p. 2.
58. At the time Corn's family came to the area, Dewey County was simply named "D County." Although present-day Dewey County has a population of fewer than five thousand, at the time of statehood about thirteen thousand people resided there (Linda D. Wilson, "Dewey County," *The Encyclopedia of Oklahoma History and Culture,* http://www.okhistory.org/publications/enc/entry.php?entry+DE018 [accessed December 31, 2019]).
59. Corn would have kept the county's records in a wood frame building in Taloga. The Dewey County Courthouse was not built until 1926 (ibid.).
60. *Oklahoman,* June 1, 1926, p. 9; June 9, 1926, p. 10. Corn had lost a highly publicized vehicular manslaughter case. During N. B. Johnson's impeachment trial, Johnson's attorney implied that Corn's resignation had resulted from bribery allegations against him (Impeachment trial of Justice N. B. Johnson [hereafter Johnson impeachment trial], May 7, 1965, p. 91).
61. *Oklahoman,* July 25, 1934, p. 1.
62. *Oklahoman,* November 8, 1928, p. 1.
63. *Oklahoman,* November 7, 1934, p. 1.
64. Testimony of Corn, *U.S. v. Cargill,* CR-65-27, vol. 5, p. 26; Berry and Alexander, *Justice for Sale,* 133–40.
65. Testimony of Corn, *U.S. v. Cargill; American Savings Life v. Loomis,* 131 P.2d 65 (Okla., 1942). A life insurance company had refused to pay a claim after the insured's death, claiming the insured had failed to disclose he had syphilis at the time he bought the policy. The Supreme Court reversed the district court and ordered a new trial, holding the judge should have instructed the jury on the defendant's theory. Corn and Welch voted with the majority, reversing the verdict in favor of Cargill's client.
66. At N. B. Johnson's impeachment trial, the defense implied that Hugh Carroll had helped Corn capitalize the small loan business. Carroll's testimony was vague on that point. When asked if he had lent Corn the money for the business, Carroll said, "Not to my knowledge" (testimony of Carroll, Johnson impeachment trial, May 6, 1954, p. 58).
67. Testimony of Felix Simmons, *U.S. v. Cargill,* Vol. 8, pp. 150–52.
68. Oklahoma Bar Association, "Report of Investigating Committee of Examiners," *Oklahoma Bar Association Journal* 35 (1965): 603.
69. Testimony of Corn, Johnson impeachment trial, May 6, 1965, p. 84.
70. Berry and Alexander, *Justice for Sale,* 73–74. In Corn's case the supernumerary position paid nine thousand dollars per year, about 60 percent of his salary on the court (*Oklahoman,* April 17, 1957, p. 1).

Chapter 2

1. *Johnson v. Johnson,* 279 P.2d 298 (Okla., 1954).
2. *Oklahoman,* August 11, 1965, p. 1. Testimony of Corn in deposition regarding Johnson will case, July 13, 1965, Maurice Merrill Papers, Western History Collections, University of Oklahoma Libraries, Norman (hereafter Maurice Merrill Papers; Johnson will

contest). Two months later, Arnold, apparently short of money, borrowed against the Cadillac.
3. Testimony of Corn, Johnson will contest, July 13, 1965. Corn's later explanation for a three-thousand-dollar cash payment on the car was that it came from the Selected Investments bribe money. However, that event had not yet occurred.
4. *Oklahoman*, June 15, 1965, p. 1; Berry and Alexander, *Justice for Sale*, 48–51.
5. *Woodson v. Huey*, 261 P.2d 199 (Okla., 1953). Justice Johnson wrote the opinion affirming the trial court; Corn, Welch, and Arnold concurred.
6. *Oklahoman*, February 18, 1966, p. 9.
7. *West Edmond Hunton Lime Unit v. Young*, 325 P.2d 1047 (Okla., 1958); *Oklahoman*, February 18, 1966, p. 9.
8. *Battle v. Mason*, 293 P.2d 324 (Okla., 1955).
9. In 1994 University of Oklahoma Law School professor Judith Maute explored the inappropriate relationship between Looney and Welch in her article "*Peevyhouse v. Garland Coal & Mining Co.* Revisited: The Ballad of Willie and Lucille," *Northwestern University Law Review* 89 (1994–1995): 1341–482. The author argues that *Peevyhouse*, a case long criticized by legal remedies scholars, may have been influenced by the close relationship between Welch and Looney and thus been decided more by favoritism than poor legal reasoning.
10. *U.S. v. Cargill*, Vol. 12, pp. 709–16.
11. Transcript of Johnson impeachment trial, pp. 98–100, 262.
12. Ibid.
13. Ben Arnold had died from a long-standing heart ailment on September 30, 1955, about two months before the opinion was published (*Oklahoman*, October 1, 1955, p. 1).
14. Marshall's testimony was confusing on this point. Cargill had once represented Marshall in oil and gas litigation in Noble County (*U.S. v. Cargill*, Vol. 8, pp. 7–19).
15. Testimony of Henry Grant Marshall, *U.S. v. Cargill*, Vol. 7, pp. 70–84. Testimony of Marshall, *State ex rel Harlan G. Grimes*, SCBD 1794, July 25, 1966, Oklahoma Department of Libraries, 29-10, Box 1, Folders 31–33 (Grimes's attempt to be reinstated to the Oklahoma Bar Association).
16. Testimony of Corn, *U.S. v. Cargill*, June 6, 1965, Vol. 4, pp. 10–11.
17. *Marshall v. Amos*, 300 P.2d 990 (Okla., 1956). Justice Davison did not join in the opinion.
18. *Oklahoman*, February 18, 1966, p. 9. Bayless resigned from the bar shortly before his scheduled disbarment proceeding.
19. Grimes had a history of suing judges and lawyers. In 1946 he had sued his client and an Oklahoma City attorney for conspiring to "cheat and defraud" him out of his fee in a federal court case. In 1948 he had sued Cargill and a Creek County judge over unpaid fees, alleging a conspiracy among Cargill, the judge, his clients, and other attorneys to misappropriate his fee (*Oklahoman*, May 26, 1945, p. 5; July 23, 1948, p. 33). He had also accused Tom Gibson, a justice defeated for reelection in 1953, of distributing twenty thousand dollars in bribe money in a case involving the Oklahoma City school system (Berry and Alexander, *Justice for Sale*, p. 45).
20. *Oklahoman*, March 10, 1959, p. 5; April 21, 1959, p. 4.

21. *Oklahoman,* March 9, 1969, p. 12. After the scandal was exposed, Grimes unsuccessfully sought reinstatement to the Oklahoma Bar Association.
22. Opening statement of Representative Burke G. Mordy and testimony of Mrs. R. D. Farmer, Johnson impeachment trial, p. 35 and pp. 116–25, respectively.
23. *Oklahoma Company v. O'Neil,* 333 P.2d 534 (Okla., 1958). Corn had not run for reelection, and Carlile had been defeated by William Berry.
24. *U.S. v. Cargill,* 65-27-CR. In 1961 Otha Westcott, Cargill's daughter, was struck and killed by a car near Cargill's ranch northwest of Oklahoma City.
25. Hunt had an unusual career on the Oklahoma bench. He had been a district judge from Tulsa, then served a term on the Supreme Court from 1925 to 1931. He later reentered the judiciary in Oklahoma County. In 1955 he returned to the Supreme Court after the death of Justice Ben Arnold but died in August 1956. His seat was filled by Lon Carlile and, later, by William A. Berry.
26. Testimony of Hugh Carroll, *U.S. v. Carroll,* June 2, 1965, Vol. 2, pp. 11–12.
27. Testimony of Corn, Johnson impeachment trial, May 6, 1955, p. 77.
28. Ibid., p. 79.
29. Berry and Alexander, *Justice for Sale,* 70–71.
30. Testimony of Corn, *U.S. v. Cargill,* Vol. 4, p. 15.
31. Carroll visited Corn in the hospital (testimony of Carroll, Johnson impeachment trial, p. 65).
32. In Oklahoma the chief justice and vice chief justice serve two-year terms, then rotate out of the position and return to their normal duties. By tradition the vice chief justice becomes chief justice. In January 1957 the Supreme Court had bypassed Vice Chief Justice and heir apparent Ben T. Williams in favor of Welch, with Corn becoming the vice chief. Welch succeeded Johnson, whose term as chief justice had expired (*Oklahoman,* January 15, 1957, p. 1).
33. *Selected Investments v. Oklahoma Tax Commission,* 309 P.2d 267 (Okla., 1957).
34. Carroll drew twenty-three thousand dollars from his personal account and two thousand dollars from a safety deposit box (testimony of Carroll, Johnson impeachment trial, pp. 54–55).
35. Testimony of Corn, Johnson impeachment trial, May 6, 1965, pp. 78–80.
36. Testimony of Paul S. Copeland, Johnson impeachment trial, May 6, 1965, pp. 78–80.
37. Testimony of Carroll, *U.S. v. Cargill,* June 2, 1965, Vol. 2, pp. 13–15; Johnson impeachment trial, May 6, 1965, p. 67. On his endorsement of the check, Carroll wrote, "Drew that $200,000 out for the purpose of purchasing 20,000 of Selected Investments stock."
38. *Oklahoman,* June 5, 1965, p. 1.
39. Testimony of Corn, *U.S. v. Cargill,* June 7, 1965, Vol. 6, pp. 13–17.
40. *Oklahoman,* January 21, 1958, p. 1.
41. *Oklahoman,* December 24, 1957, p. 1.
42. Ibid.
43. *Oklahoman,* January 3, 1958, p. 1.
44. *Oklahoman,* January 4, 1958, p. 1.
45. *Oklahoman,* January 5, 1958, p. 1. Less than a week later, Gary forced Ross to resign (*Oklahoman,* January 11, 1958, p. 1).

46. Testimony of Carroll, *U.S. v. Cargill*, Vol. 2, June 2, 1965, pp. 20–22.
47. Ibid., 17–19.
48. *Oklahoman*, January 8, 1958, p. 1.
49. *Oklahoman*, January 9, 1958, p. 1.
50. *Oklahoman*, January 14, 1958, p. 1; February 11, 1958, p. 1. As a federal judge Bohanon proved to be a judicial activist, ordering students bused to integrate the Oklahoma City schools and forcing reform in Oklahoma's prison system. For more information on Bohanon's career, see Jace Weaver, *Into the Rock Let Me Fly: Luther Bohanon and Judicial Activism* (Norman: University of Oklahoma Press, 1993).
51. *Oklahoman*, February 28, 1958, p. 1; March 4, 1958, p. 1.
52. Judge Lee R. West, "Biographical Sketch for the Historical Society of the Tenth Circuit on Judge Stephen R. Chandler," static1.squarespace.com, 4b00eba52a2db00/t/5 4515543e4b09d0d07d0b22b/1414620755682/Chandler,bio.pdf (accessed December 31, 2019).
53. Berry and Alexander, *Justice for Sale*, 2–3.
54. *New York Times*, Chandler obituary, April 29, 1989, p. 10; West, "Biographical Sketch," 11–17.
55. West, "Biographical Sketch," 6–15.
56. *Oklahoman*, March 8, 1958, p. 1; March 9, 1958, p. 1.
57. Julia Carroll, who had been a longtime employee of Selected Investments, had married Hugh in 1952 after the death of Carroll's first wife (Testimony of Julia Carroll, *U.S. v. Carroll*, June 4, 1965, Vol. 3).
58. Testimony of Hugh Carroll, *U.S. v. Cargill*, June 2, 1965, Vol. 2, pp. 23–24.
59. The name "Pierre Laval" may have been taken from a French politician from the Vichy years, who was executed after World War II for Nazi collaboration (see Weaver, *Into the Rock*, 62).
60. *Oklahoman*, March 18, 1958, p. 1.
61. *Oklahoman*, July 17, 1964, p. 3.

Chapter 3

1. Scales and Goble, *Oklahoma Politics*, 301–3.
2. J. Howard Edmondson Papers, Oklahoma Department of Libraries, Oklahoma City, Oklahoma.
3. Scales and Goble, *Oklahoma Politics*, 313–25.
4. Ibid., 327–33.
5. Bob Burke, *How Bad It Was, How Good It Is: The Value of an Independent Oklahoma Judiciary* (Oklahoma City: Commonwealth Press, 2015). The source of the tip was never revealed.
6. Author's interview with Judge John Amick (retired), March 2, 2017. Amick went on to a long and distinguished career as an Oklahoma County district judge.
7. Interview with B. Andrew Potter, *Oklahoman*, June 25, 1965, p. 1.
8. *United States v. Corn*, Western District of Oklahoma, 64-85-CR, July 1, 1964.
9. Corn statement to authorities, December 9, 1964, pp. 75–77 (Maurice Merrill Papers).
10. *Oklahoman*, January 21, 1964, p. 5.
11. *Oklahoman*, April 7, 1964, p. 1; April 8, 1964, p. 1; April 9, 1964, p. 1; April 10, 1964, p. 1.

12. In addition to his 1957 cancer surgery, Corn had suffered a serious heart attack in 1962.
13. *Oklahoman,* April 24, 1965, p. 1.
14. *United States v. N. S. Corn,* 64-85-CR, July 1, 1964.
15. Ibid.; interview with B. Andrew Potter, *Oklahoman,* June 25, 1965, p. 1.
16. *Oklahoman,* July 2, 1964, p. 1; July 3, 1964, p. 5.
17. *Oklahoman,* December 1, 1963, p. 1.
18. *Oklahoman,* April 13, 1964, p. 27.
19. *Oklahoman,* July 3, 1964, p. 5.
20. *Oklahoman,* July 5, 1964, p. 5.
21. Testimony of Floyd Rheam, Johnson impeachment trial, May 10, 1965, pp. 209–11; testimony of Rheam, *United States v. O. A. Cargill,* Vol. 10, June 11, 1965.
22. *Oklahoman,* July 19, 1964, p. 1.
23. *Oklahoman,* August 25, 1964, p. 1; August 26, 1964, p. 1. Welch, who had been indicted, and Johnson, not yet a publicly named suspect, both voted for extending subpoena power to the committee.
24. *Oklahoman,* September 5, 1964, p. 1; September 9, 1964, p. 1.
25. *United States v. Corn,* 64-85CR, July 29, 1964; *Oklahoman,* July 30, 1964, p. 1.
26. Although the grand jury that indicted Welch and Corn had sat in Oklahoma City, which is in Oklahoma's federal western district, Welch provided proof that he had been a registered voter in Pushmataha County since 1913. At Welch's request the trial was therefore moved to the eastern district, based in Muskogee.
27. *Oklahoman,* November 13, 1969, p. 39.
28. For a description of the exploitative nature of Indian land sales during these years, see Angie Debo, *And Still the Waters Run* (Princeton, N.J.: Princeton University Press, 1940).
29. *Muskogee Times Democrat,* October 15, 1964.
30. Testimony of Fern Welch and Martha Ann Ellis, *U.S. v. Welch,* appeal summary, 75–77.
31. *Oklahoman,* June 15, 1932, p. 4; July 8, 1932, p. 4. See also Scales and Goble, *Oklahoma Politics,* 167–75.
32. Interview of Earl Welch, 1958, Oklahoma Historical Society Oral History Living Legends, Oklahoma Historical Society. Welch later became president of the Inter-Tribal Council of the Five Civilized Tribes.
33. One of Welch's sons developed a debilitating mental illness. Welch and his wife also spent considerable money on another son's education. However, domestic situations like this were hardly unique to the Welch family.
34. Defendant's summary of case, *U.S. v. Welch,* citing *Tulsa Tribune,* October 8, 1964.
35. Testimony of William Strawbridge, *U.S. v. Welch,* trial summary, p. 58. In 1962 Welch called Strawbridge to assess Strawbridge's interest in repurchasing the home.
36. *Oklahoman,* October 8, 1964, p. 1.
37. *Oklahoman,* December 18, 1958, p. 39; July 7, 1959, p. 21.
38. *Oklahoman,* October 9, 1964, p. 1; *U.S. v. Welch,* trial transcript, 476.
39. *U.S. v. Welch,* trial transcript, 478.
40. *Oklahoman,* October 9, 1964, p. 1.

41. *Norman Transcript*, October 6, 1964, p. 1.
42. Citing Corn's precarious health, Harper allowed Corn to stay in a hotel, rather than being housed in jail (*Oklahoman*, October 10, 1964, p. 1).
43. *Oklahoman*, October 13, 1964, p. 1.
44. *Oklahoman*, October 20, 1964, p. 1.
45. *U.S. v. Welch*, 27158-CR, Eastern District of Oklahoma, sentencing hearing, November 13, 1964.
46. *McAlester News-Capital*, November 13, 1964, p. 1.
47. *Oklahoman*, October 21, 1964, p. 1.
48. *Oklahoman*, October 23, 1964, p. 1.
49. *Norman Transcript*, October 20, 1964, pp. 1, 2.
50. *Oklahoman*, July 7, 1964, p. 12; October 6, 1964, p. 13; *Tulsa Tribune*, October 26, 1964, p. 8.
51. *Norman Transcript*, October 13, 1964, pp. 1, 2; October 30, 1964, pp. 4, 20; *Daily Ardmoreite*, November 1, 1964, p. 26.
52. *Norman Transcript*, October 13, 1964, p. 1.
53. *Enid Daily Eagle*, November 2, 1964.
54. Neither Harris nor Wilkinson campaigned on the issue of SQ 415. The Senate campaign focused more on personalities than issues, with Wilkinson emphasizing his people skills and Harris his close ties to the Democratic president.
55. *Oklahoman*, November 4, 1964, p. 1.
56. *Oklahoman*, November 11, 1964, p. 2.
57. *Tulsa Tribune*, November 10, 1964, p. 10.
58. *Oklahoman*, August 18, 1974, p. 1.
59. *McAlester News Capital*, November 12, 1964, p. 1; *Tulsa Tribune*, November 10, 1964, p. 1; November 18, 1964, p. 1.
60. *Oklahoman*, December 1, 1964, p. 1. For the most part, Welch, even though he continued to be paid, did not participate in court business after his indictment.
61. Burke, *How Bad It Was*, 10–14.
62. Affidavit of James H. Harrod, December 31, 1964 (Maurice Merrill Papers, Western History Collection, University of Oklahoma).
63. *Oklahoman*, December 20, 1964, p. 1.
64. *Oklahoman*, January 6, 1965, p. 1.
65. Burke, *How Bad It Was*, 14.

Chapter 4

1. *Oklahoman*, January 6, 1965, p. 1.
2. *Oklahoman*, January 8, 1965, p. 1.
3. *Colegrove v. Green*, 328 US 549 (1946).
4. J. Douglas Smith, *On Democracy's Doorstep: The Inside Story of How the Supreme Court Brought "One Person, One Vote" to the United States* (New York: Hill and Wang, 2014), 52–98.
5. *Baker v. Carr*, 369 US 186 (1962).
6. Smith, *On Democracy's Doorstep*, 213.
7. *Reynolds v. Sims*, 377 US 533 (1964).

8. Smith, *On Democracy's Doorstep*, 225.
9. Ibid., 235.
10. Ibid., 218–40.
11. Ibid., 241–62.
12. Ibid., 263–80.
13. *Oklahoman*, June 18, 1963, p. 32.
14. Robert B. Bingham, *Reapportionment of the House of Representatives: Politics and Process* (Norman, OK: Legislative Research Series, Bureau of Government Research, 1971), 2–3.
15. Samuel A. Kirkpatrick, *The Legislative Process in Oklahoma: Policy Making, People, and Politics* (Norman: University of Oklahoma Press, 1972), 35–39.
16. Bingham, *Reapportionment of the House of Representatives*, 2–6; Scales and Goble, *Oklahoma Politics*, 328–30.
17. Scales and Goble, *Oklahoma Politics*, 337.
18. Gary W. Copeland and Jean G. McDonald, "Reapportionment and Partisan Competition: When Does Reapportionment Matter?," *Political Behavior* 9, no. 2 (1987): 160–73; Kirkpatrick, *Legislative Process in Oklahoma*, 35–39.
19. Berry and Alexander, *Justice for Sale*, 18–19.
20. Ibid., 1–6. The roles of Berry and Chandler did not become public knowledge until the 1996 publication of Berry's memoir.
21. *New York Times v. Sullivan*—the U.S. Supreme Court case that required plaintiffs who were public figures to prove actual malice in libel and slander suits—had been decided the previous year, but libel and slander laws were still considered powerful weapons.
22. Berry and Alexander, *Justice for Sale*, 22–25.
23. Ibid., 36, 39.
24. Ibid., 37–38.
25. *Oklahoman*, January 22, 1965, p. 5.
26. *Oklahoman*, February 16, 1965, pp. 1, 24.
27. *Oklahoman*, February 20, 1965, p. 4.
28. *Oklahoman*, February 23, 1965, p. 1.
29. The next day Justice Johnson also declined the polygraph offer.
30. *Oklahoman*, March 11, 1965, pp. 1, 10.
31. *Oklahoman*, March 17, 1965, p. 1.
32. *Oklahoman*, May 2, 1962, p. 1. Ingle also mentioned a disturbing conversation he had several years previously with Tom Waldrep, a former state senator and disbarred attorney, regarding a completely different case, *Independent-Eastern Torpedo v. Price*, 258 P.2d 189 (Okla., 1953). Waldrep claimed to have paid Welch ten thousand dollars for a favorable result in the case, which involved an oilfield injury. Johnson wrote the opinion, with which Welch concurred. Corn and Arnold dissented. Waldrep's name also appeared in a case involving Welch's brother, Lee, an attorney who claimed to have paid Waldrep, who had been disbarred for many years, ten thousand dollars to assist in a brief. During his career, Waldrep, who died in 1959, had been jailed for selling state jobs as a state senator, disciplined for embezzling from a guardianship estate, and charged with attempting to bribe the Pottawatomie County attorney to

allow gambling at a Shawnee club (*Oklahoman*, August 5, 1955, p. 1; October 9, 1959, p. 8; July 9, 1942, p. 1).

33. *Oklahoman*, March 22, 1965, p. 1; March 23, 1965, pp. 1, 12. In his letter Welch complained of the use of hearsay evidence against him and what he perceived as the unfairness of the impeachment process. He did not mention his federal criminal conviction.
34. *Oklahoman*, March 25, 1965, p. 1; March 30, 1965, p. 1.
35. *Oklahoman*, March 28, 1965, p. 1.
36. *Oklahoman*, April 6, 1965, p. 1; April 7, 1965, p. 1.
37. Johnston had lost control of the legislature, been unresponsive and aloof, and had alienated conservative senators with his endorsement of Al Smith in the 1928 Democratic presidential race. He was convicted on one count of general incompetence in office (Scales and Goble, *Oklahoma Politics*, 135–53).
38. *Oklahoman*, March 23, 1965, p. 13.
39. *Oklahoman*, April 9, 1965, p. 3.
40. *Oklahoman*, April 13, 1965, p. 1.
41. Testimony of N. B. Johnson, Johnson impeachment trial, transcript, 223–24.
42. N. B. Johnson Papers, Oklahoma Historical Society, Oklahoma City, Oklahoma.
43. Bayless returned to the practice of law and became a figure in the Oklahoma bribery scandal.
44. Representative Burke Mordy, Johnson impeachment trial, opening statement, 32.
45. Porter, a lawyer, had become the first African American elected to the Oklahoma State Senate after court-ordered redistricting the previous year.
46. Johnson impeachment trial, 56–69.
47. Ibid., 76–115.
48. Ibid., 143–61.
49. Ibid., 234.
50. Ibid., 240–41.
51. Ibid., 262.
52. Eight hundred dollars in 1958 was the equivalent of $6,944.34 in 2018. Two thousand dollars in 1958 dollars would be worth $17,360.85 in 2018.
53. Questions from Senators Ted Findeiss, Richard Stansberry, and John Garrett, Johnson impeachment trial, transcript, May 11, 1965, 286.
54. In his argument Green called N. S. Corn "an evil old man who admits he has lived a life of corruption" (*Oklahoman*, May 9, 1965, p. 1).
55. Johnson impeachment trial, 401–3.
56. These included Clem Hamilton from Poteau, Leroy McClendon from Atoka, Gene Stipe from McAlester, and John Massey from Durant. Southeastern Oklahoma was so heavily Democratic that Republican governor Bellmon could not find a suitable Republican from the district to replace Earl Welch. He eventually appointed Ralph Hodges from Durant, who served for many years.
57. Johnson impeachment trial, transcript, 401–3.
58. *Oklahoman*, July 22, 1965, p. 3.
59. Ibid. Foreman had represented high-profile criminal defendants for years. A few years later, he would represent alleged Martin Luther King Jr. assassin James Earl

Ray, persuading Ray to plead guilty. The wisdom and propriety of that decision remain in question today.
60. *Oklahoman,* May 2, 1965, p. 1.
61. *Oklahoman,* June 2, 1965, p. 1.
62. *Oklahoman,* June 3, 1965, p. 1.
63. *Oklahoman,* June 4, 1965, p. 1.
64. Justices Harry Halley, Denver Davison, and W. H. Blackbird immediately called a press conference to deny Corn's claim. The next day the Oklahoma Bar Association issued a statement announcing it had cleared the three justices, pointing out Corn had previously testified he had no knowledge of any wrongdoing by them, and noting this statement had purportedly come from Cargill, who was being prosecuted for lying under oath. Other than Cargill's dubious statement to Corn, no evidence exists of any inappropriate conduct by these justices (*Oklahoman,* June 5, 1965, p. 1; June 6, 1965, p. 1).
65. As noted earlier, at Cargill's suggestion Corn had retained Oklahoma City tax attorney John Speck to represent him in his tax troubles. For undisclosed reasons, Corn had a heated argument with Speck and Cargill and discharged Speck (Testimony of John Speck, *U.S. v. Cargill,* vol. 10, pp. 296–99).
66. Harrod visited Corn's home on December 31, 1964, during Harrod's last week in office. It is unclear whether Harrod's promise was enforceable, but no state charges were filed against Corn.
67. *U.S. v. Cargill,* 65-27-CR, vol. 7, pp. 62–64; *Oklahoman,* June 5, 1965, p. 1.
68. *U.S. v. Cargill,* 65-27-CR, vol. 7, 8, 9, and 11; *Oklahoman,* June 9, 1965, p. 1.
69. *Oklahoman,* June 12, 1965, p. 1. The next day Haffa was served with a million-dollar lawsuit filed by two Oklahoma City attorneys who had represented Amos. The lawyers claimed they would have received large fees if Amos had won. They claimed they had lost the fees because Haffa helped bribe the justices (ibid.).
70. Ibid.
71. Cargill did not explain why he would be involved in the selection of a chief justice, a procedure normally conducted within the court.
72. *U.S. v. Cargill,* vol. 11, 500–503.
73. Ibid., vol. 11, pp. 588–602.
74. Ibid.
75. *Oklahoman,* June 15, 1965, p. 1.

Chapter 5

1. Henry Bellmon, *The Life and Times of Henry Bellmon* (Tulsa, Okla.: Council Oak Books, 1992), 201–2.
2. *Oklahoman,* November 9, 1966, p. 1.
3. *Oklahoman,* April 16, 1965, p. 1.
4. *Oklahoma Journal,* September 12–13, 1964, p. 1. Until the previous week, Atkinson had been actively pursuing his own defamation suit against the Oklahoma Publishing Company, which he was forced to dismiss after the U.S. Supreme Court's decision in *New York Times v. Sullivan* (*Oklahoma Journal,* September 4, 1964, p. 1).

5. *Oklahoman*, September 15, 1964, p. 1; September 17, 1964, p. 3.
6. *Oklahoman*, July 29, 1965, p. 1.
7. The racing bill did not pass the House of Representatives in 1961.
8. *Oklahoman*, July 29, 1965, p. 1.
9. *Oklahoman*, April 2, 1959, p. 1.
10. Murray returned to Oklahoma after living in Fort Worth, Texas, for a few years, where he had worked for an oil well servicing company and a limousine service. State Senator Gene Stipe suggested Murray come back to Oklahoma, where he eventually finished his career as an attorney for the Oklahoma Department of Public Welfare (Dowell, "Murray, Johnston"); *Oklahoman*, April 26, 1960, p. 4.
11. In 1966, at the height of his legal troubles, Pate changed parties and ran as a Republican for Carl Albert's congressional seat. His campaign was not taken seriously, and he was resoundingly defeated.
12. *Oklahoman*, September 5, 1965, p. 1; September 6, 1965, p. 19.
13. *Oklahoma City Times*, June 8, 1965, p. 1.
14. *Oklahoman*, March 11, 1965, p. 10.
15. *Oklahoman*, February 29, 1972, p. 29. The arthritis drug trial ended in a hung jury.
16. *Oklahoman*, August 3, 1965, p. 3.
17. *Oklahoman*, August 10, 1965, p. 1; August 20, 1965, p. 1.
18. Judge McInnis, a Democrat, was defeated by her Republican opponent in the 1966 election. The next year she was tragically murdered by her estranged husband at her downtown Oklahoma City law office (*Oklahoman*, June 20, 1967, p. 1).
19. Pate also had the dubious distinction of being the subject of two simultaneous grand jury inquiries. In a less important case, a Leflore County grand jury investigated claims that Pate's brother Pat, the Leflore County attorney, had required his secretary to do secretarial work for Whit and another private attorney on county time. No indictment resulted (*Oklahoman*, December 7, 1965, p. 1).
20. *Oklahoman*, December 31, 1965, p. 1.
21. *Oklahoman*, May 25, 1966, p. 1.
22. Charles H. Sheldon, "Influencing the Selection of Judges: The Variety and Effectiveness of State Bar Activities," *Western Political Quarterly* 30, no. 3 (September 1977): 397–400.
23. Mary Lyle Weeks, "Chapter Four," *Sooner Magazine*, Summer 1994, pp. 12–16.
24. Phillip Simpson, "The Modernization and Reform of the Oklahoma Judiciary," *Oklahoma Politics*, October 1994, p. 6.
25. *Norman Transcript*, October 6, 1964, p. 1.
26. *Oklahoman*, November 16, 1966, p. 1.
27. Sneed was also a candidate to succeed George L. Cross as president of OU and had the backing of outgoing governor Henry Bellmon. J. Herbert Holliman was selected instead (*Oklahoman*, November 16, 1966, p. 1).
28. Henry Bellmon letter to John McCune, February 17, 1965, Bellmon Papers, Oklahoma State University, Box 39, File 3.
29. *Oklahoman*, December 3, 1965, p. 1; October 29, 1966, p. 1.
30. Simpson, "Modernization and Reform of the Oklahoma Judiciary," 10.
31. *Oklahoman*, June 15, 1966, p. 3; August 4, 1966, p. 1; August 24, 1966, p. 1.

32. *Oklahoman,* October 19, 1966, p. 1; October 21, 1966, p. 3; October 28, 1966, p. 1. Thomas left Oklahoma in 1971 to write editorials for the *Pittsburgh Post-Gazette,* where he worked for thirty years (Dan Majors, "Obituary: Clarke M. Thomas / Longtime PG Editorial Writer and Senior Editor," *Pittsburgh* [Pa.] *Post-Gazette,* February 23, 2009, https://www.post-gazette.com/news/obituaries/2009/02/23/Obituary-Clarke-M-Thomas-Longtime-PG-editorial-writer-and-senior-editor/stories/200902230169).
33. John David Rausch, "Initiative and Referendum," *The Encyclopedia of Oklahoma History and Culture,* https: www.okhistory.org/publications/enc/entry.php?entry=IN025 (accessed December 31, 2019); Charles A. Beard, "The Constitution of Oklahoma," *Political Science Quarterly* 24, no. 1 (March 1909): 95–114.
34. *Oklahoma City Times,* November 4, 1966, p. 10.
35. *Oklahoman,* November 8, 1966, p. 3.
36. *Oklahoman,* November 1, 1966, p. 1.
37. *Oklahoman,* March 10, 1967, p. 42.
38. *Oklahoman,* April 26, 1967, p. 1.
39. *Oklahoman,* August 13, 1966, p. 1; August 17, 1966, p. 3.
40. Democrat Andy Payne had been elected statewide to the office of Supreme Court clerk eight times and had held the office for thirty-two years. In 1928 Payne had attracted national attention by winning the Trans-Continental footrace from Los Angeles to New York, averaging running sixty miles per day (*Oklahoman,* September 16, 1966, p. 4).
41. *Oklahoman,* October 29, 1966, p. 1. Only nine of the thirty members were present for the vote, which took place at approximately 10 P.M. on a Friday.
42. *Oklahoman;* March 3, 1966, p. 1.
43. *Oklahoman,* March 1, 1966, p. 1; March 2, 1966, p. 23.
44. *Oklahoman,* May 5, 1966, p. 1.
45. *Oklahoman,* March 6, 1966, p. 1.
46. *Oklahoman,* May 5, 1966, p. 1.
47. *Oklahoman,* May 4, 1966, p. 1.
48. *Oklahoman,* May 25, 1966, p. 1.
49. Preston Moore obituary, *Oklahoman,* September 2, 2004, https://obits.oklahoman.com/obituaries/oklahoman/obituary.aspx?n=preston-jay-moore&pid=2573491.
50. *Oklahoma City Times,* November 7, 1966, p. 1.
51. *Oklahoma City Times,* November 1, 1966, p. 24.
52. *Tulsa Daily World,* November 3, 1966, p. 2; November 5, 1966, p. 3. The ads were sponsored by a organization calling itself the Citizens for Good Government Committee.
53. *Tulsa Daily World,* November 1, 1966, p. 6.
54. *Oklahoman,* May 10, 1966, p. 1; October 14, 1966, p. 8; October 21, 1966, p. 1.
55. *Tulsa Daily World,* November 3, 1966, p. 3.
56. *Oklahoman,* October 14, 1966, p. 9.
57. Ray Parr, "Parr for the Course," *Oklahoman,* September 11, 1966, p. 12.
58. *Oklahoman,* November 1, 1966, p. 1.
59. *Oklahoman,* November 2, 1966, p. 1.
60. *Oklahoma City Times,* November 4, 1966, p. 3.

61. *Oklahoman*, November 9, 1966, p. 8.
62. *Oklahoma City Times*, November 4, 1966, p. 11; November 5, 1966, p. 5.
63. *Tulsa Daily World*, November 9, 1966, p. 1.
64. *Oklahoman*, October 25, 1966, p. 4; *Oklahoma City Times*, November 5, 1966, p. 5.
65. *Oklahoman*, November 4, 1966, p. 3.
66. Otis Sullivant, *Oklahoman*, November 19, 1966, p. 2.
67. *Tulsa Daily World*, November 9, 1966, p. 1; November 2, 1966, p. 3; November 12, 1966, p. 18; *Oklahoma City Times*, November 7, 1966, p. 12.
68. Travis Walsh, *Tulsa Daily World*, November 13, 1966, p. 1.
69. Otis Sullivant, *Oklahoman*, November 10, 1966, p. 3.

Chapter 6

1. Otis Sullivant, *Oklahoman*, January 22, 1967, p. 4.
2. *Oklahoman*, November 10, 1966, p. 1; November 11, 1966, p. 1; December 20, 1966, p. 4; *Tulsa Daily World*, November 11, 1966, p. 1.
3. Dewey Bartlett, January 10, 1967, State of the State Address, Bartlett Papers, Oklahoma Department of Libraries, Oklahoma City, Oklahoma.
4. *Oklahoman*, April 12, 1967, p. 1; July 9, 1967, p. 1.
5. *Oklahoman*, March 22, 1967, p. 1; April 12, 1967, p. 1.
6. *Oklahoman*, August 20, 1967, p. 1.
7. *Muskogee Times-Democrat*, January 3, 1967, p. 1.
8. Otis Sullivant, *Oklahoman*, March 26, 1967, p. 26.
9. Otis Sullivant, *Oklahoman*, April 11, 1967, p. 4.
10. Otis Sullivant, *Oklahoman*, April 21, 1967, p. 3.
11. *Oklahoman*, April 26, 1967, p. 1.
12. Otis Sullivant, April 25, 1967, p. 7.
13. *Oklahoman*, May 8, 1967, p. 1.
14. *Oklahoman*, May 9, 1967, p. 1; May 12, 1967, p. 1.
15. *Oklahoman*, May 9, 1967, p. 1.
16. *Oklahoman*, May 20, 1967, p. 4.
17. *Durant Daily Democrat*, May 18, 1967, p. 6.
18. Otis Sullivant, *Oklahoman*, May 14, 1967, p. 3.
19. *Oklahoman*, June 22, 1967, p. 17.
20. John Young, letter to the editor, *Oklahoman*, May 22, 1967, p. 14.
21. *Oklahoman*, July 7, 1967, p. 8; *Duncan Banner*, July 6, 1967, p. 1.
22. Ray Parr, "Parr for the Course," *Oklahoman*, July 9, 1967, p. 25.
23. *Medford Patriot-Star*, June 20, 1967, p. 1.
24. *Duncan Banner*, July 9, 1967, p. 1.
25. Ray Parr, "Parr for the Course," *Oklahoman*, July 9, 1967, p. 25.
26. *Marietta Monitor*, July 7, 1967, p. 7.
27. *Oklahoman*, July 10, 1967, p. 19.
28. Oklahoma State Election Board official results, Oklahoma City, Oklahoma.
29. 1960 U.S. Census, Oklahoma, https://www2..census.gov/library/publications/decennial/1960/population-volume-1/37749254v1p38ch.2.pdf (accessed December 31, 2019).

30. *Durant Daily Democrat,* May 11, 1967, p. 1.
31. *Oklahoman,* January 3, 1968, p. 1.
32. *Oklahoman,* March 19, 1968, p. 39.
33. *Oklahoman,* March 1, 1968, p. 1; March 6, 1968, p. 1.
34. George B. Fraser, "Oklahoma's New Judicial System," *Oklahoma Law Review* 21 (1968): 373–410, at 380. The authority granted to special district judges has been increased over the years.
35. *Oklahoman,* March 8, 1968, p. 3. The Court of Civil Appeals has since been expanded to twelve judges: six in Oklahoma City and six in Tulsa.
36. Fraser, "Oklahoma's New Judicial System," 402.
37. *Oklahoman,* August 1, 1968, p. 17.
38. *Oklahoman,* August 4, 1968, p. 16.
39. *Oklahoman,* September 6, 1968, p. 1; September 12, 1968, p. 1.
40. *Tulsa Tribune,* September 13, 1968, p. 52.
41. *Tulsa Tribune,* September 14, 1968, p. 24.
42. *Tulsa Tribune,* September 12, 1968, p. 56.
43. *Tulsa Tribune,* September 16, 1968, p. 13.
44. *Tulsa Tribune,* September 5, 1968, p. 1.
45. *Tulsa World,* September 9, 1968, p. 6; September 15, 1968, p. 1.
46. *Tulsa World,* September 12, 1968, p. 1; September 24, 1968, p. 1; September 15, 1968, p. 1.
47. *Tulsa Tribune,* September 6, 1968, p. 2.
48. *Tulsa Tribune,* September 18, 1968, p. 38.
49. *Oklahoman,* September 18, 1968, p. 1.
50. Opala interview, p. 6.
51. Burke and Leonard, *Opala* , 123–35.

Chapter 7

1. *Oklahoman,* October 30, 1968, p. 8; March 11, 1969, p. 7.
2. *Oklahoman,* January 29, 1974, p. 4; April 4, 1975, p. 51.
3. 20 O.S. Sec. 1658. The strengthening of the statute apparently was in response to the actions of Richard Hovis, an associate district judge from Hobart, who was found guilty of inappropriate sexual conduct toward female employees and removed from the bench. Hovis repeatedly discussed his case with the media (*Oklahoman,* August 30, 1997, p. 1).
4. Records of Court on the Judiciary, CJTD 75-2 (*Oklahoman,* November 23, 1975, p. 1; November 1, 1977, p. 51).
5. Records of the Oklahoma Court on the Judiciary (*Oklahoman,* October 21, 1977, p. 13; October 27, 1977, p. 13; July 12, 1978, p. 19).
6. Records of the Oklahoma Court on the Judiciary (*Oklahoman,* October 21, 1977, p. 13; October 27, 1977, p. 13).
7. Records of Oklahoma Court on the Judiciary (*Oklahoman,* July 31, 1988, p. 87; September 9, 1988, p. 1).
8. *Oklahoman,* June 18, 1994, p. 1.
9. *Oklahoman,* January 13, 2002, p. 11A; February 11, 2012, p. 1A.

10. Petition for Removal, *State of Oklahoma ex. rel. Douglas Combs v. Curtis DeLapp*, Court on the Judiciary, CJTD 2018-1, *Oklahoman*, August 21, 2018, p. 1.
11. *Oklahoman*, February 16, 2011, p. 13W.
12. Constitution of the State of Oklahoma, Article VII-B, section 3.
13. *Oklahoman*, March 17, 2019, p. 1; April 18, 2019, p. 1; Tres Savage, "Bills Seek to Modernize 1967 Supreme Court District Map," *NonDoc*, February 18, 2019, https://nondoc.com/2019/02/18/modernizing-1967-supreme-court-district-map/.
14. *Republican Party of Minnesota v. White*, 536 US 765 (2002).
15. *Citizens United v. Federal Election Commission*, 558 US 310 (2010).
16. James L. Gibson, *Electing Judges: The Surprising Effects of Campaigning on Judicial Legitimacy* (Chicago: University of Chicago Press, 2012); Chris W. Bonneau and Melinda Gann Hall, *In Defense of Judicial Elections* (New York: Routledge, 2009); Melinda Gann Hall, *Attacking Judges: How Campaign Advertising Influences State Supreme Court Elections* (Stanford, Calif.: Stanford University Press, 2015).
17. Gibson, *Electing Judges*, 141.
18. Jed Handelsman Shugerman, *The People's Courts: The Rise of Judicial Elections* (Cambridge, Mass.: Harvard University Press, 2012).
19. Shugerman, *The People's Courts*, Kindle edition, location 3648–56.
20. Adam Liptak, "Motion Ties W. Virginia Justice to Coal Executive," *New York Times*, January 15, 2008, http://nytimes.com/2008/01/15us/15court.html.
21. Justice Benjamin served twelve years on the court but was defeated for reelection in 2016, garnering only 12 percent of the vote. In 2015 West Virginia changed its method of selection of justices to nonpartisan election. Don Blankenship was convicted of a misdemeanor charge of conspiring to violate mine safety and health standards in relation to a mine explosion in which twenty-nine miners died. He served one year in federal prison. In 2018 he unsuccessfully ran for the Republican nomination for the U.S. Senate. Fearing Blankenship's controversial reputation, President Donald Trump endorsed Blankenship's opponent for the Republican nomination.
22. *Caperton v. A.T. Massey Coal Co.*, 556 US 868 (2009).
23. As of 2018 the West Virginia Supreme Court has completely fallen apart. The Republican legislature impeached all five members of the Supreme Court for excessive spending on their chambers, waiting several months in order to ensure that the Republican governor would be able to appoint their successors. A Democratic justice resigned, then pled guilty to wire fraud. A Republican justice was convicted of multiple counts of fraud and false statements but refused to leave the bench. Another Democratic justice resigned rather than face impeachment, while a Republican justice was tried before the Senate and acquitted. The chief justice, a Democrat, challenged the legality of her impeachment; that case went to, of all places, the West Virginia Supreme Court, comprising five acting justices, which ruled against the legislature (Mark Joseph Stern, "West Virginia's Absurd, Dangerous Supreme Court Impeachment Crisis," *Slate*, October 12, 2018, https://slate.com/news-and-politics/2018/10/west-virginia-supreme-court-impeachment-constitutional-crisis.html).
24. Shugerman, *The People's Courts*, Kindle location 3526–30. Texaco's lawyers had also donated to the Supreme Court races, but in lesser amounts.

25. Editorial Board, "Judges Shouldn't Be Partisan Punching Bags," *New York Times*, April 8, 2018.
26. Jack N. Hays, "Oklahoma Moves Forward in Judicial Selection," *Tulsa Law Review* 6, no. 2 (1970): 97–98.
27. A. G. Sulzberger, "In Iowa, Voters Oust Judges Over Marriage Issue," *New York Times*, November 3, 2010; Michael Curriden, "Judging the Judges: Landmark Iowa Elections Send Tremor through the Judicial Retention System," *ABA Journal*, January 1, 2011, http://www.abajournal.com/magazine/article/landmark_iowa_elections_send_tremor_through_judicial_retention_system.
28. The Oklahoma Civil Justice Council, an arm of the Oklahoma Chamber of Commerce, evaluates justices of the Supreme Court on their perceived friendliness toward business and whether their decisions "have had the effect of restraining the spread of liability." See https://okciviljustice.com.
29. *Oklahoman*, August 12, 2018, p. 4, https://oklahoman.com/5604410/new-super-pac-targeted-oklahoma.
30. Oklahoma State Election Board records, https://www.ok.gov/elections/support/10gen.html.
31. Shugerman, *People's Courts*, Kindle edition, location 3730.

Bibliography

Archives
Bartlett, Dewey F. Papers. Oklahoma Department of Libraries. Oklahoma City, Oklahoma.
Bellmon, Henry Louis. Papers. Oklahoma State University Library—Special Collections, Stillwater, Oklahoma.
Edmondson, J. Howard. Papers. Oklahoma Department of Libraries. Oklahoma City, Oklahoma.
Gary, Raymond. Papers. Oklahoma Department of Libraries. Oklahoma City, Oklahoma.
Johnson, N. B. (Napoleon Bonaparte). Papers. Oklahoma Historical Society, Oklahoma City, Oklahoma.
Merrill, Maurice. Papers. Western History Collections, University of Oklahoma Libraries, Norman.
Oklahoma State Election Board official records. Oklahoma City, Oklahoma.
Opala, Marian P. Papers. Oklahoma Hall of Fame, Oklahoma City, Oklahoma.

Newspapers
Daily Oklahoman, Oklahoma City
Daily Ardmoreite, Ardmore
Durant Daily Democrat
Lawton Constitution
Medford Patriot-Star
Muskogee Phoenix
Norman Transcript
Oklahoma City Times
Oklahoma Journal (Oklahoma City)
Tulsa Tribune
Tulsa World

Judicial Proceedings
Impeachment proceedings of Justice N. B. Johnson. Oklahoma State Senate, May 1965.
State ex rel. Oklahoma Bar Association v. Harlan G. Grimes, SBCD 1794. Oklahoma Department of Libraries, Oklahoma City, Oklahoma.
United States v. O. A. Cargill. United States District Court for the Western District of Oklahoma. National Archives and Records Administration. Fort Worth, Texas.
United States v. N. S. Corn. United States District Court for the Western District of Oklahoma. CR-65-85. National Archives and Records Administration. Fort Worth, Texas.

United States v. Earl Welch. United States District Court for the Eastern District of Oklahoma. National Archives and Records Administrations, Fort Worth, Texas.

Books

Albert, Carl, and Danney Goble. *Little Giant: The Life and Times of Speaker Carl Albert.* Norman: University of Oklahoma Press, 1990.

Bellmon, Henry. *The Life and Times of Henry Bellmon.* Tulsa, Okla.: Council Oak, 1992.

Bensel, Richard Franklin. *The Political Economy of American Industrialization, 1877–1900.* Cambridge: Cambridge University Press, 2000.

Berry, William A., and James Edwin Alexander. *Justice for Sale: The Shocking Scandal of the Oklahoma Supreme Court.* Oklahoma City: Macedon, 1996.

Bingham, Richard D. *Reapportionment of the Oklahoma House of Representatives: Politics and Process.* Norman: Legislative Research Series, Bureau of Government Research, University of Oklahoma, 1972.

Blight, David W. *Race and Reunion: The Civil War in American Memory.* Cambridge, Mass.: Belknap Press of Harvard University Press, 2001.

Bonneau, Chris W., and Melinda Gann Hall. *In Defense of Judicial Elections.* New York: Taylor & Francis, 2009.

Brinkley, Alan. *The End of Reform: New Deal Liberalism in Recession and War.* New York: Vintage Books, 1995.

Broder, David S. *Democracy Derailed: Initiative Campaigns and the Power of Money.* New York: Harcourt, 2000.

Bryant, Keith L. *Alfalfa Bill Murray.* Norman: University of Oklahoma Press, 1968.

Buchanan, James Shannon, and Edward Everett Dale. *A History of Oklahoma.* Evanston, Ill.: Row, Peterson, and Company, 1924.

Burke, Bob. *How Bad It Was, How Good It Is: The Value of an Independent Oklahoma Judiciary.* Oklahoma City: Commonwealth Press, 2015.

Burke, Bob, and Ryan Leonard. *Opala: In Faithful Service to the Law.* Oklahoma City: Oklahoma Heritage Association, 2012.

Callender, Clarence. *American Courts: Their Organization and Procedure.* New York: McGraw-Hill, 1927.

Cargill, O. A. *My First 80 Years.* Oklahoma City: Banner Books, 1965.

Caro, Robert A. *Means of Ascent: The Years of Lyndon Johnson.* New York: Vintage Books, 1990.

Carter, Dan T. *The Politics of Rage: George Wallace, the Origins of the New Conservatism, and the Transformation of American Politics.* Baton Rouge: Louisiana State University Press, 1995.

Cash, W. J. *The Mind of the South.* New York: Vintage Books, 1941.

Casey, Orben J. *And Justice for All.* Oklahoma City: Oklahoma Heritage Association by Western Heritage Books Inc., 1989.

Chang, David A. *The Color of the Land: Race, Nation, and the Politics of Landownership in Oklahoma, 1832–1929.* Chapel Hill: University of North Carolina Press, 2010.

Cockburn, J. S. *A History of English Assizes, 1558–1714.* Cambridge: Cambridge University Press, 1972.

Cronin, William. *Nature's Metropolis: Chicago and the Great West.* New York and London: W. W. Norton and Company, 1991.
Debo, Angie. *And Still the Waters Run.* Princeton, N.J.: Princeton University Press, 1940.
Dorman, Robert L. *Alfalfa Bill: A Life in Politics.* Norman: University of Oklahoma Press, 2018.
Dubois, Philip L. *From Ballot to Bench: Judicial Elections and the Quest for Accountability.* Austin: University of Texas Press, 1980.
Dubois, W. E. B. *Black Reconstruction in America.* Oxford: Oxford University Press, 2014 (originally published in 1935).
Foner, Eric. *Reconstruction: America's Unfinished Revolution, 1863–1877.* New York, Harper & Row, 1988.
Foreman, Grant. *A History of Oklahoma.* Norman: University of Oklahoma Press, 1942.
Franklin, Buck Colbert. *My Life and an Era: The Autobiography of Buck Colbert Franklin.* Baton Rouge: Louisiana State University Press, 2000.
Gibson, Arrell Morgan. *Oklahoma: A History of Five Centuries.* 2nd ed. Norman: University of Oklahoma Press, 1981 (first ed. 1965).
Gibson, Arrell Morgan, ed. *Frontier Historian: The Life and Word of Edward Everett Dale.* Norman: University of Oklahoma Press, 1975.
Gibson, James L. *Electing Judges: The Surprising Effects of Campaigning on Judicial Legitimacy.* Chicago: University of Chicago Press, 2012.
Goble, Danney. *Progressive Oklahoma: The Making of a New Kind of State.* Norman: University of Oklahoma Press, 1980.
Hall, Melinda Gann. *Attacking Judges: How Campaign Advertising Influences State Supreme Court Elections.* Stanford, Calif.: Stanford University Press, 2015.
Hale, Grace Elizabeth. *Making Whiteness: The Culture of Segregation in the South, 1890–1940.* New York: Vintage Books, 1998.
Hart, James S. *The Rule of Law, 1603–1660.* Harlow, England: Pearson Education Limited, 2003.
Hauan, Martin. *How to Win Elections without Hardly Cheatin' at All.* Oklahoma City: Midwest Political Publications, 1983.
Hofstadter, Richard. *The Age of Reform.* New York: Vintage Books, 1955.
Institute of Judicial Administration. *The Justice of the Peace Today.* New York, Institute of Judicial Administration, New York University, 1965.
James, Howard. *Crisis in the Courts.* New York: David McKay Company, 1971.
Key, V. O., Jr. *Southern Politics in State and Nation.* Knoxville: University of Tennessee Press, 1977 (originally published in 1949).
Kilpatrick, Samuel A. *The Legislative Process in Oklahoma: Policy Making, People, & Politics.* Norman: University of Oklahoma Press, 1978.
Leuchtenburg, William E. *The Perils of Prosperity, 1914–1932.* Chicago: University of Chicago Press, 1993 (originally published in 1958).
Limerick, Patricia Nelson, Clyde A Milner II, and Charles E. Rankin. *Trails toward a New Western History.* Lawrence: University of Kansas Press, 1991.
Scales, James R., and Danney Goble. *Oklahoma Politics: A History.* Norman: University of Oklahoma Press, 1982.

Schlesinger, Arthur M., Jr. *The Coming of the New Deal, 1933–1935*. New York: Houghton Mifflin, 1986 (originally published in 1958).

Shugerman, Jed Handelsman. *The People's Courts: Pursuing Judicial Independence in America*. Cambridge, Mass.: Harvard University Press, 2012.

Skyrme, Thomas. *The History of Justices of the Peace*, 3 vols. Chichestershire, England: Countrywide Press, 1991.

Smith, J. Douglas. *On Democracy's Doorstep: The Inside Story of How the Supreme Court Brought "One Person, One Vote" to the United States*. New York: Hill and Wang, 2014.

Straub, Matthew J., ed. *Running for Judge: The Rising Political, Financial, and Legal Stakes of Judicial Elections*. New York: New York University Press, 2007.

Tindall, George Brown. *The Emergence of the New South, 1913–1945*. Baton Rouge: Louisiana State University Press, 1967.

Turner, Frederic Jackson. *The Frontier in American History*. London: Pearl Necklace Books, 2015 (originally published as an essay in 1893).

Thompson, John. *Closing the Frontier: Radical Response in Oklahoma, 1889–1923*. Norman: University of Oklahoma Press, 1986.

Weaver, Jace. *Then to the Rock Let Me Fly: Luther Bohanon and Judicial Activism*. Norman: University of Oklahoma Press, 1996.

White, Richard. *The Middle Ground: Indians, Empires, and Republics in the Great Lakes Region, 1650–1815*. New York: Cambridge University Press, 1991 (reprinted 2011).

Wickett, Murray R. *Contested Territory: Whites, Native Americans, and African Americans in Oklahoma, 1865–1907*. Baton Rouge: Louisiana State University Press, 2000.

Williamson, Joel. *The Crucible of Race: Black-White Relations in the American South since Emancipation*. New York: Oxford University Press, 1984.

Woodward, C. Vann. *Tom Watson: Agrarian Rebel*. New York: Oxford University Press, 1963 (originally published in 1938).

Woodward, C. Vann. *Origins of the New South*. Baton Rouge: Louisiana State University Press, 1951, 1971.

Woodward, C. Vann. *Thinking Back: The Perils of Writing History*. Baton Rouge: Louisiana State University, 1986.

Articles

Avery, Michael K., and Ronald M. Peters Jr. "Oklahoma's Statutory Constitution." *Oklahoma Politics* 13 (November 2004): 47–63.

Beard, Charles A. "The Constitution of Oklahoma." *Political Science Quarterly* 24, no. 1 (1909): 95–114.

Boyer, Larry M. "The Justices of the Peace in England and America from 1506 to 1776: A Bibliography." *Quarterly Journal of the Library of Congress* 34, no. 4 (October 1977): 315–26.

Curriden, Mark. "Judging the Judges: Landmark Iowa Elections Send Tremor through the Judicial Retention System." *American Bar Association Journal*, January 1, 2011, www.abajournall.com/magazine/article/landmark-iowa-elections-send-tremor-through-judicial-retention-elections.

Darcy, R. "Conflict and Reform: Oklahoma Judicial Elections, 1907–1998." *Oklahoma City University Law Review* 26 (Summer 2001): 519–48.

Fraser, George B. "Oklahoma's New Judicial System." *Oklahoma Law Review* 21, no. 4 (November 1968): 373–410.
Hackney, Sheldon. "*Origins of the New South* in Retrospect." *Journal of Southern History* 38, no. 2 (May 1972): 191–216.
Hays, Jack N. "Oklahoma Moves Forward in Judicial Selection." *Tulsa Law Journal* 6 (1969): 85–89.
Hays, Jack N. "Selection of Judges in Oklahoma." *Tulsa Law Journal* 2 (1965): 127–35.
Orejal, Keith. "What Does C. Vann Woodward's *Origins of the New South* Have to Say to the Twenty-First-Century Reader?" September 8, 2014. https: //tropicsofmeta.com/2014/09/08/what-does-woodwards-origins-of-the-new-south-have-to-say-to-the-first-time-reader.
Sheldon, Charles H. "Influencing the Selection of Judges: The Variety and Effectiveness of State Bar Activities." *Western Political Quarterly* 30, no. 3 (September 1977): 397–400.
Simpson, Philip. "The Modernization and Reform of the Oklahoma Judiciary." *Oklahoma Politics,* October 1994, 1–14.
Simpson, Philip. "The Role of Partisanship in the Reform of the Oklahoma Judiciary." *Oklahoma Politics,* October 1996, 1–16.
Weeks, Mary Lyle. "Chapter Four: When the Sneeds and the Thompsons Gathered for OU Law Commencement 1994, Family Tradition and University History Intertwined Once Again," *Sooner Magazine,* summer 1994, 12–16.

Dissertation

Scales, James Ralph. *Political History of Oklahoma, 1907–1949.* Diss. University of Oklahoma, 1949.

Internet Sources

Encyclopedia of Oklahoma History and Culture, Oklahoma Historical Society, www.okhistory.org.

Index

References to illustrations appear in italic type.

AFL-CIO (American Federation of Labor–Congress of Industrial Organizations), 103–4

African Americans: and Claude Chandler lynching, 19–20; and legislature in 1965, 66–67; and E. Melvin Porter, 73, 76, 141n45; and segregation, 8; and Tulsa Race Massacre, 20

Alford, Roy, Cargill and, 20–21

Alito, Samuel, 123

Allard, Lou, 72

Allen, Font, 26

American Bar Association (ABA), 15, 86

American Savings Life v. Loomis, 22

Amick, John, 41, 137n6

Anderson, William L., 100–101

Arnall, Sue Ann, 126

Arnold, Ben: and Cargill, 20, 80, 142n71; and Corn, 27, 135n13; death of, 3

Atkinson, W. P. (Bill), 40, 82, 93–94

Baker v. Carr, 7, 63. *See also* U.S. Supreme Court

Bartlett, Dewey: and advocacy of Judicial Nomination commission, 100, 128; background of, 94; campaign of 1966, 92, 95; and court reform, 104, 113; inactive in special election, 105; inauguration of, 100; in opposition to silent vote, 50; and Sneed plan neutrality, 110

Bass-Lesure, Tammy, 118

Battle v. Mason. See Meadors will case

Bayless, Wayne, 26, 73, 141n43

Bellmon, Henry: backs Sneed plan, 111; Blankenship warned by, 6; first Republican governor (1962), 6, 40; and judicial reform committee, 87; and Operation Giant Stride, 62; scandal kept in public eye by, 128; validation of 1962 victory, 97–98; watchdog panel appointed by, 44

Benjamin, Brent, 121–22, 147n21

Berry, William A.: on Carlile, 31; Corn's statement revealed by Judge Chandler, 67, 140n20; on ex parte discussion by lawyers, 14–15; Judge Chandler's meeting with, 66–67; scandal revealed to Blankenship by, 67–68; Welch incident, 66

Biden, Joe, 124

Bingaman, George, 72–75

Black, Hugo, 63

Blackbird, W. H., 28, 42–43

Blackstock, Leroy, 87–88, 93, 111–12

Blankenship, Don, 122

Blankenship, G. T., *52*; Corn statement revealed to, 67–68, 140n21; first Republican Oklahoma attorney general, 52, 96; scandal exposed by, 5–6, 68, 128

Bohanon, Luther, 35–36, 137n50

Bonneau, Chris W., 120–21

Booker, Cory, 124

Brennan, William, 63

Brown, Elvin, 111, 117

Bryan, William Jennings, 2

Bullard, James, 88

Burns, J. Phil, 33, 34, 38, 39

155

Camp, John N. (Happy), 92, 93
campaign of 1966, 92–98; governor's race, 92–93; and Nix, 92–93; overwhelming Republican victories, 96, 97; and Republican party progress, 92; results consistent with nationwide trend, 97; State Question 431 approved, 93; way cleared for court reform, 98
Cannon, Joe, 117
Cargill, O. A., 53; background of, 3, 19–20, 133n51, 133n53; Claude Chandler lynching and, 20; and Corn, 30–32, 41, 51, 52, 128, 136n23; and corruption, 25, 26, 68; denial of "Pierre Laval" knowledge, 79–80; Fifth Amendment invoked by, 71; Foreman as defense attorney, 71; indictment of, 68; as "Mister X," 5, 68; and Nance bribe offer, 27; as Selected Investment's attorney, 34–35; unsavory reputation of, 2, 20–21, 133n56. See also Cargill perjury trial
Cargill perjury trial: Cargill cross-examination by Kline, 80; Cargill's wife's testimony, 79; Cargill testimony, 79–80; Carroll as prosecution witness, 77; Corn as prosecution witness, 78, 142n64, 142n65; Fleming as prosecution witness, 80; Foreman as defense attorney, 77–80; and guilty verdict, 80; Haffa's testimony, 79, 142n69; and Judge Harper, 77; Marshall's testimony, 78–79; Nance as prosecution witness, 80; sentencing by Harper, 80; and Zwifel's testimony for defense, 79. See also Cargill, O. A.; Foreman, Percy
Carlile, W. A. "Lon," 27, 31, 66
Carroll, Hugh, 54; assets frozen, 37; background of, 3; and bribery scheme, 30–32; and Corn relationship, 73; Corn's story confirmed by, 76; exploitation by, 2; immunity granted to, 70;

incarceration of, 38, 39; legislative committee addressed by, 18, 133n43; and J. Murray's campaign, 17–18; as prosecution witness, 73–74; after release from prison, 40–41; and Selected Investments, 15, 136n37; and Welch trial testimony, 47
Carroll, Julia (Mrs. Hugh), 54; and objection to "Pierre Laval" story, 37–38, 137n57; statement by, 41; testimony in Cargill perjury trial, 77
Castle, Forest, 82
Chandler, Claude, lynching of, 19–20
Chandler, Stephen: background as federal judge, 36–37; and continuance denial for Carroll, 79–80; and Corn's statement, 66–67, 140n20; and O'Bryan, 37, 41. See also Berry, William A.
Citizens United v. Federal Election Commission, 120
Clark, Tom, 63
Colbert, Tom, 125
Colegrove v. Green, 62–63
Collins, Everett, 82, 84
Combs, Douglas, 118, 125
Connor, James W., 72, 111–12
constitutional amendments (1967), 3–4, 102–3
Cook, Dale, 43–44
Cope, Milton B.: investigator with distrust of Selected Investments, 16–17; and prejudice charged by Carroll, 19; replaced by Ross, 18, 34, 133n43
Corn, Lonnie (son of Nelson), 33
Corn, Nelson Smith, 55; *American Savings Life v. Loomis* and, 22, 134n65; and Arnold, 27; background of, 13, 21–23, 134nn58–60; bribe in *Selected Investments* appeal, 67; bribe money returned by, 34; and bribery scheme, 30–33; and Cargill, 21, 22, 28, 67, 128; confession statement of, 5, 6, 66–67, 140n20; and confidentiality agreement, 51, 52; and corruption, 25;

exploitation by, 2, 22–23; immunity granted to, 70, 78; and IRS, 41; and N. B. Johnson, 74; parole of, 51; as prosecution witness, 74; retirement of, 23; and Selected Investments, 18, 23; and *Selected Investments* case, 74; small-loan business interests and, 22–23, 134n66; testimony as bargaining chip, 50–51; and Welch implicated by, 47, 67, 74. *See also* Corn, Nelson Smith, prosecution of

Corn, Nelson Smith, prosecution of, 40–44; conviction and sentencing, 42; Corn's bribery revealed by Potter, 42; disbarment by OBA, 43; federal grand jury indictment of, 41–42; imprisonment of, 44; Judge Harper and, 42; pleadings to court, 42, 138n12; resignation from office, 42–43. *See also* Corn, Nelson Smith

Council on Judicial Complaints: establishment of, 115; and secrecy of operation, 115–16, 146n3. *See also* Court on the Judiciary

county attorney system, 11–12

Court of Appeals, establishment of, 109, 146n35

Court of Criminal Appeals, 101; abolishment under Sneed plan, 88; creation of, 12, 13; Judge Lile removed from, 118; and legislative plan, 91, 101; and Nix, 92–93, 125; Pate's appeal to, 85

Court on the Judiciary, 115–18; accountability to voters provided by, 127; and Bass-Lesure and Olmstead, 118; and Brown acquittal, 117; and compulsory retirement of judges, 117; Council on Judicial Complaints formed, 115–16; and DeLapp case, 118; effectiveness of, 118; and first judge removed in 1968, 115; and Graham case, 116–17; and Haworth case, 116, 117; and Lile case, 118; and political power brokering, 117; and Sullivan case, 116, 117; and Thompson resignation before trial, 118. *See also* Council on Judicial Complaints

court reform, aftermath of, 115–29; overview, 115; Court on the Judiciary, 115–18; Judicial Nominating Commission and judicial selection, 118–24; results of reform and factors in its passage, 127–29; retention ballot and nonpartisan trial judge elections, 124–27

court system, 9–14; county attorney system, 11–12; courtrooms busy, 12, 132n23; distrust of, 14–15; election of judges, 12, 132n27; failure to meet ABA standards, 15; and nominating district, 13; partisanship of judges, 13–14; Supreme Court, 12, 132nn25–26. *See also* Court of Criminal Appeals

Cox, Archibald, 63

Criminal Court of Appeals, 12, 21. *See also* Court of Criminal Appeals

Crowe, V. P., 47

Cunningham, Robert O., 38

Daily Oklahoman, supports Sneed plan, 88–89

Dallet, Rebecca, 124

Davison, Denver, 28

DeLapp, Curtis, and removal petition, 118

Dirksen, Everett, and reapportionment, 64

Doenges, William, and J. Murray's campaign, 17–18

Douglas, Paul, 64

Douglas, William O., 63, 64

Duncan, Paul, 36, 37, 38

Eagleton, James, 42

Edmondson, Drew, 125

Edmondson, James, 125

Edmondson, J. Howard: court reform ignored by, 39–40; election as governor begins voter restiveness, 40, 128; and legislature's resistance to

158 INDEX

Edmondson, J. Howard (*continued*)
plans, 40; and Pate as legal counsel, 82, 83; reapportionment favored by, 64–65; reform platform of, 39
ex parte discussion by lawyers, prevalence of, 14–15

Fallin, Mary, 119
Fleming, Laura, 26, 80
Foreman, Percy: Cargill's defense attorney, 71; and Corn cross-examination by, 78; as defense attorney, 141n59. *See also* Cargill perjury trial
Fourteenth Amendment, 63
Fowler, Dick, 51
Frankfurter, Felix, 62–63
Freeman, Harold, 100–101

Garrison, Denzil, 111–12
Gary, Raymond: and campaign of 1966, 92–93, 94; Carlile appointed to court by, 31; defeated by Atkinson, 40; reapportionment blocked by, 64–65
Gee, Robert, 102
Geyh, Charles Gardner, 121
Gibson, James L., on partisan judicial elections, 120–21
Goldwater, Barry, 49
Gourley, Leland, 92
Graham, Gar, 116–17
Grantham, Roy, 56; and Bingaman, 74; and Corporation Commission scandal investigation, 101; and Council on Judicial Complaints, 115–16; and dissent on court reform proposals, 91; impeachment trial presiding officer, 71; state senator, 18
Green, Fred, attorney for Johnson, 72
Grey, Earl, 79
Grimes, Harlan: disbarment of, 6, 28–29; Johnson accused of bribery by, 75; *Marshall v. Amos* bribery accusations by, 6, 28–29, 135n19, 136n21. See also *Marshall v. Amos*
Gurich, Noma, 119

Haffa, Titus, 27, 79, 142n69
Hale, Clyde, Jr., 100–101
Hale, Clyde, Sr., 100
Hall, David, 92
Hall, Melinda Gann, and partisan judicial elections, 120–21
Halley, Harry, 27, 28
Halley, Harry (justice), 13–14
Hamm, Harold, 126
Haralson, Howard R., 126
Harkey, Paul, 18
Harper, Roy, 41–42, 44, 47–48
Harris, Curtis: and Blankenship, 68; and dog-racing bribery claim, 84; and grand jury investigation announced by, 69–70
Harris, Fred R.: reelection in 1966, 96; and Sneed, 86; and Bud Wilkinson, 49, 90, 139n54
Harrod, James: and Carroll statement, 41; and Corn, 50–51, 78, 142n66; grand jury probe announced by, 43–44; and Woolsey story, 82
Haworth, Bill, 116, 117
Hedges, Harold, 34
Henry, Brad, 119
Holder, Eric, 124
Howard, Gene, 116
Hunt, Albert, 29–30, 136n25

impeachment proceedings, 70–75, 140n32; Carroll as prosecution witness, 73–74; Corn as prosecution witness, 74; Fifth Amendment invoked by Cargill, 71; Ingle's testimony in, 70–71, 140n32; N. B. Johnson impeached on two counts, 71; N. B. Johnson testimony in own defense, 74–75; senators sworn in as jurors, 71–72; and Welch denials, 70; and Welch's resignation from court, 71, 141n33
impeachments, history of, 72
Ingle, R. O., 70–71, 75, 140n32

Jackson, Floyd, 27
Jamail, Joe, and Pennzoil, 123

Johnson, Dexter G., 25–26
Johnson, Lyndon, 49
Johnson, Napoleon Bonaparte (N. B.), 57; accusation of bribery by Grimes, 75; background of, 3, 72–73; bribes accepted by, 5, 28, 30; and conviction, 75–76, 141n56; Corn's evidence against, 68; financial records as undoing, 74–75, 76, 141n52; impeached on two counts, 71; impeachment recommended by committee, 71; impeachment trial of, 18; suspension from office, 71, 128; testimony in impeachment trial, 74–75
Johnson v. Johnson, 25–26, 27
Johnston, Henry S., 7, 72, 141n37
Jones, Roy, 100–101
Judicial Nominating Commission: controversy over, 101–2; criticisms today, 4; establishment of, 3; opposition to, 104; qualified lawyers ensured by, 114
Judicial Nominating Commission and judicial selection: and constitutional amendment (2010), 119; and demographic change in Supreme Court (2019), 120; and drawbacks to appellate judicial elections, 124; under fire from legislature, 118–19; *Massey* case on partisan judicial elections, 122–23; and partisan elections versus merit selection, 120–22; and Supreme Court rulings, 118–19; and Texas's judicial campaigns, 123; and Wisconsin Supreme Court election, 124
judicial nomination commissions, 86
Judicial Reform Inc., 87–88
judicial selection. *See under* Judicial Nominating Commission and judicial selection
justice of the peace (JP): abolishment of office, 4, 10–11, 101, 114, 132n17; continued use of, 24; functions of, 9–10; and rural communities, 108; and Sneed, 86–87

Katzenbach, Nicholas D., 78
Kelly, D. L., 26
Kennedy, John F., 63
Kennedy, Anthony, 123
Kennedy, Robert F., 42
Kerr, Robert S., 73
Key, V. O., Jr., 6–7
Kline, David, 80
Kuehn, Dana, 125
Ku Klux Klan, 7, 8, 20

lawyer-legislators: banning of by Graham, 116–17; as opportunists, 8, 109; reform and, 2–3; and Selected Investments, 18–19
League of Women Voters, 88, 89, 104, 110
legislative reform (1967): and annual session length, 101; and appellate judge selection, 101–2; conference committees reach agreement, 102–3; court reform issues submitted to people, 103; and fed-up voters, 99; judicial reform stalled in senate, 101; and passage of constitutional amendments, 3–4, 102–3; Sneed plan problematic, 102. *See also* Grantham, Roy; Oklahoma Corporation Commission
legislature (1968), 108–10; and court reforms, 109–10, 146n34, 146nn34–35; and entrenched rural judges, 110; and teacher pay increase debate, 108–9
Lewis, Bob, 83
Lile, Steve, 118
Looney, Ned, 20, 26–27, 80, 135n9

Marshall, H. G., 27–28, 78–79
Marshall v. Amos: bribery proved in, 3; and Cargill's scheme, 27–29, 78; and Corn, 6, 67, 74; subpoenas issued in, 69–70. *See also* Grimes, Harlan
Massad, Anthony, 91

Massey case on partisan judicial elections, 122–23, 147n21, 147n23
Massey Coal Company, 122
Maynard, Elliott, 122
McBride, Willard, 50
McCarty, J. D., 58; challenge by Democratic legislature, 128; and defeat in 1966, 95–96, 99, 128; and defeat of judicial reform, 113; denial of legislative bribery by, 85; Edmondson and, 40; and grand jury investigation, 84–85; indictment of, 96; and J. D. McCarty Center, 97; leadership style of, 81; as Speaker of the house, 6, 18; speculation about, 97, 128; Welch impeachment opposed by, 50, 62; and Woolsey's dog-racing bribery claim, 82–83
McCune, John, 87, 111–12
McGraw, Warren, 122
McInnis, Jo Ann, 85, 143n18
McSpadden, Clem, 50, 76, 87–88
Meadors, C. F., 26–27
Meadors will case, 3, 14, 16–27
Merrill, Maurice, 43, 86–87
Miskovsky, George, 18, 77
Missouri plan. *See* Sneed plan for legislative reform
"Mister X," 5, 68
"money bills," 85
Monnet, Melinda, 117
Moore, Preston: background of, 92, 93–94; and court reform, 94–95, 128; and JP court, 97
Mordy, Burke G.: chief counsel for house investigating committee, 60, 72; and Corn investigation, 74; sparring match with Welch, 70
Mothersead, O. B, 18
Murrah, A. P., 36
Murray, Johnston, 17–18, 29, 45
Murray, William H. "Alfalfa Bill," 17
Murray School of Agriculture (now Murray State College), 17
Myers, Ruby, and Welch, 45–46

Nance, James, 27, 80
Neal, Linwood, 33, 34–35
Nesbitt, Charles, 90, 92–93
Nix, Kirksey, 92–93, 124–25. *See also under* Court of Criminal Appeals
Nixon, Richard, 92
nonpartisan ballot in judicial elections: and incumbency, 125–26; state judicial system respected by voters, 126–27

OBA. *See* Oklahoma Bar Association (OBA)
O'Bryan, W. H. (Pat), 37, 41
Odom, Jack, 104
Oklahoma: demographics of, 8, 107–8, 120, 131n7; early, 1–2; legislature in first fifty years, 7–8; malapportionment ranking of, 64; one-party state, 6–7, 129; ripe for corruption, 24; and segregation, 8. *See also* court reform, aftermath of
Oklahoma Bar Association (OBA): active role in reform by, 44, 129, 138n23; and Corn, 43; and Corporation Commission scandal, 101; and Judicial Nominating Commission, 119; and Nix, 92–93; and Pate, 84; subpoena power granted to, 44, 138n23
Oklahoma City Times, supports Sneed plan, 88–89
Oklahoma Company, 29
Oklahoma Company v. O'Neil: bribery proved in, 3; and Corn's statement, 74, 78; and Johnson bribe, 71, 76
Oklahoma Corporation Commission: Democratic nomination runoff for, 110; and McCarty, 81; and Pate, 84; and scandal, 100–101. *See also* legislative reform (1967)
Oklahoma Democratic Party, 104
Oklahoma Education Association, 49
Oklahoma Institute for Justice Inc., 43
Oklahoma Natural Gas (ONG), 100–101

Oklahoma Republican Party, 104
Oklahoma Securities Commission, 18, 133n42
Oklahoma Supreme Court, 61; *Battle v. Mason* (Meadors case), 26–27; center of corruption in 1950s, 1, 6, 14, 25; Corn testimony in *Johnson v. Johnson*, 25–26, 134n2, 135n3; deficiencies in judicial network revealed by scandal, 127; demographics changed by legislature (2019), 120; and other influence peddlers, 26–27; and Sneed plan failure, 113. *See also* Selected Investments *entries*
Oklahoma Tax Commission: and Pate's tax records, 85; and Selected Investments, 3, 29, 32, 33
Oklahoma Tax Commission v. Selected Investments, 29; bribery proved in, 3
Olmstead, Wayne, resignation of, 118
Opala, Marian: background of, 113; and centralization of court funding, 114; death of, 119; first court administrator, 113
Operation Giant Stride, Bellman's proposal for, 62

Parr, Ray, on skepticism of special election, 105–6
Pate, Whit: career of, 83–84, 143nn10–11; immunity granted to, 85, 143n19; indictment of, 85; subpoenaed by McCarty grand jury, 84–85; and Woolsey's dog-racing bribery claim, 82–83
Pendergast, Tom, 86
Pennzoil, 123
"Pierre Laval" story: and Cargill, 69, 77, 79–80; and Carroll, 66, 73–74; and Julia Carroll's testimony, 77, 79; fictional French-Canadian oilman, 37–38, 40, 137n59
Pope, Charles, 76
Porter, E. Melvin, 73, 76, 141n45
Potter, B. Andrew, 40–41, 42, 51

Privett, Rex: and Bartlett rift, 109; against judicial nomination commission, 102; Speaker succeeding McCarty, 99–100
Prohibition, repeal of, 39–40
prosecution and reform, 39–51; overview, 39–40. *See also* Corn, Nelson Smith, prosecution of; State Question 415; Welch, Earl, trial of

racing bill legislation, 83, 143n7
Reagan, Ronald, 92
reapportionment, legislative: changes in 1965 legislature, 65–66; and federal court supervision of Oklahoma (1965), 65; and Gary, 64–65; killed by silent vote, 65; malapportionment in Oklahoma, 64; significance of, 76; and U.S. Supreme Court controversy, 62–65
reform proposals (1966), 85–92; and annual session of legislature amendment approved, 85–86, 101; and Judicial Reform Inc., 87–88; and Sneed plan, 85–86. *See also* Blackstock, Leroy; Sneed, Earl; Sneed plan for legislative reform
reform results: deficiencies in judicial network revealed by scandal, 127; increased professionalism in judiciary, 127, 129. *See also* Court on the Judiciary
Reif, John, 125
Republican Party of Minnesota v. White, 120
retention ballot for appellate judges, 124–25, 148n28
Reynolds v. Sims, 63
Rheam, Floyd, 43, 74
Rigg, William, 38
Rinehart, James, Selected Investments attorney, 17, 18
Roberts, John, 123
Rogers, Cleeta John, 92
Rogers, John, 89–90
Romang, Richard, 76
Roosevelt, Franklin D., 13

Ross, Herschal K.: background of, 16; Cope replaced by, 18, 34, 133n43; criticisms of by legislature, 33–34
Ross, Ronald (son), 34

Scalia, Antonin, 120, 123
Screnock, Michael, 124
segregation, 8
Selected Investments: Carroll as founder, 15; expansion of, 19; factors leading to exposure of scandal, 128; influence bought by, 18–19; investment bond program of, 16; and Murray's campaign, 17–18; and *Oklahoma Tax Commission v. Selected Investments*, 29; precarious position of, 17
Selected Investments, bankruptcy of, 33–38; assets frozen, 37; Cargill as attorney for, 34–35; Carroll's notice to investors, 33; and fictitious "Pierre Laval," 37–38, 137n59; Judge Chandler and, 36; and receivership, 35; recovery of money for investors, 38, 39; securities commission hearing, 34–35
Selected Investments v. Oklahoma Tax Commission, ruling on, 32
Sharpe, Glenn, first judge removed from office, 112, 115
Sherman, Nathan S., 72
Shirk, George, 35
Shugerman, Jed Handelsman, 121
silent vote, 49–50, 65
Smalley, Phil, 72
Smith, Al, 7, 12–13, 22
Smith, James V., 96
Smith, Vondel, 95, 96
Sneed, Earl: and activism in court reform, 129; background of, 86, 143n27; chair of judicial reform committee, 87
Sneed plan for legislative reform, 85–86; ads in opposition to judicial reform, 106; backers spur victory for legislative plan, 114; delays of until 1968, 89–90; and League of Women Voters, 104; as problematic for legislators, 102–3; proposed appellate court reforms, 90–91, 143n40; proposed changes to judiciary, 88, 90; and signature drive problems, 88–89; state questions passed as alternative to, 106–7; two competing court reform proposals, 91–92; and urban-rural fissure, 107–8
Sneed plan special election, 110–14; backing and endorsements for, 110–11; and Bartlett neutrality, 110; election of judges key to failure, 113; and flaw in plan, 112; opposition to plan, 111–12; popularity of plan, 111; reasons for plan's failure, 112–13; rejection of plan, 112, 129; State Question 441 on runoff ballot (1968), 110–12
Sokolosky, Jerry, 99
special election (1967), 103–8; and Bartlett's absence from, 105; and changing demographics, 107–8; complexity of, 103; and lack of public interest in, 105–6; and Oklahoma Bar Center meeting, 105; and State Questions 447 and 448, 103–6
Speck, John, 41
state of the court, 25–38; overview, 25–27; *Marshall v. Amos* and the Westcotts, 27–29; Selected Investments' bankruptcy, 33–38; *Selected Investments* decision, 29–33
State Question 415: described, 48; failure of, 49–50; preparation of, 43; problems with passage of, 48–49
State Question 431 (establishing court on judiciary), 93
State Question 441 (Sneed plan), 110–12
Stewart, Potter, 63
Stipe, Gene, accused of bribery by Pate, 84
Sullivan, Sam, 116
Sullivant, Otis, 104
Sunray DX, 101
Swindall, Charles, 22

Swinton, Barbara, 125
system in need of reform, 5–24; overview, 5–6; distrust of court, 14–15; fifty years after statehood, 6–8. *See also* Blankenship, G. T.; Cargill, O. A.; Corn, Nelson S.; court system

Taylor, Ophia and W. S., 45–46
television allowed in senate, 72
Tenth Circuit Court of Appeals, 36, 70
Terrill, Al, 76
Texaco, 123, 142n24, 147
Texas judicial campaigns, 123
Texas Supreme Court, 123
Thomas, Clarke, 87, 88–89, 110, 144n32
Thomas, Elmer, 36, 73
Thomas, Justice, 123
Thompson, Donald, resignation of, 117
Tower, John, 92
Truman, Harry, 41, 73
Trump, Donald, 124
Tulsa Race Massacre, 20

U.S. Supreme Court: and *Citizens United v. Federal Election Commission*, 120; and Judge Chandler, 37; and reapportionment, 7, 62–65; and *Republican Party of Minnesota v. White*, 120; and Sharpe, 115; and Sneed defeat, 112

Walton, Jack, 7
Warren, Earl, 63
Washington, Paul, 33
Welch, Earl, 59; background of, 3, 44–45; Bellman's call for impeachment of, 48, 50; bribes accepted by, 5, 28, 30, 31; as chief justice, 32–33, 136n32; continued on public payroll after conviction, 50, 66, 139n60; and Corn prosecution, 43; denials of guilt, 7; federal grand jury indictment of, 41–42; and law license suspension, 50; and Looney, 26–27, 135n9; money squandered by, 32–33; resigns office, 71, 128, 141n33; and supernumerary judgeship, 23; and tax return release objection, 69
Welch, Earl, trial of, 44–48; conviction and sentencing, 47; divorce and remarriage, 46; facts withheld from jurors in, 46–47; frugality of early life with wife Fern, 45; IRS and, 46; member of Chickasaw Nation, 45, 138n32; and Ruby Myers, 45–46; trial in Muscogee (October 1964), 44, 138n26; weak prosecution case, 46–47
Welch, Fern (wife of Earl), 41, 45
Welch, James, 100–101
Westcott, Harold, 27, 29
Westcott, Otha: Cargill's daughter, 27, 29, 79, 136n24. *See also Oklahoma Company v. O'Neil*
Wheeler, John, 26
Whittaker, Charles Evans, 63
"Why Judicial Elections Stink" (Geyh), 121
Wilkinson, Bud, 49, 90, 111
Williams, Ben T., 27, 80, 135n13
Williams, G. W., 76
Winchester, Jim, 125
Wisconsin Supreme Court election, endorsements in, 124
Woolsey, Muriel Luther (Jack), 82–83

Young, John, 76, 104

Zwifel, Merle, 79

www.ingramcontent.com/pod-product-compliance
Lightning Source LLC
Chambersburg PA
CBHW031454160426
43195CB00010BB/976